THOUGHTS IN THE
WILDERNESS

J. B. PRIESTLEY

THOUGHTS IN THE
WILDERNESS

KENNIKAT PRESS
Port Washington, N. Y./London

THOUGHTS IN THE WILDERNESS

Copyright 1957 by J. B. Priestley
Reissued in 1971 by Kennikat Press by arrangement
Library of Congress Catalog Card No: 76-132090
ISBN 0-8046-1418-0

Manufactured by Taylor Publishing Company   Dallas, Texas

ESSAY AND GENERAL LITERATURE INDEX REPRINT SERIES

CONTENTS

INTRODUCTION

One of the oldest and thinnest excuses for publishing a book is the suggestion that you are doing it at other people's request, pleasing them and not yourself. Nevertheless, it is a fact that I did not consider putting these polemical pieces into a book until a great many persons, belonging to various nationalities, asked me directly or wrote to me inquiring when such a book would be appearing. Often in far-away places they had read some of the pieces in the *New Statesman and Nation*, knew there were others they had missed, and so asked for a book of them. I can only hope now, first, that they have not lost interest, and secondly, that having retained their interest they are not disappointed. Polemical pieces, originally written to challenge and provoke the readers of a weekly review, do not always reprint well: sometimes it is as if a man were shouting in a drawing-room. On the other hand, there are some drawing-rooms a man wants to shout in, and perhaps England is beginning to seem like one of them.

One of our poets told a friend of mine in New York that I had a second-rate mind. I could not share my friend's indignation at this pronouncement. I *have* a second-rate mind, and so has this poet. First-rate minds are very rare, and I have never pretended to possess one. But, over and above a few tricks of expression, I have two assets of some value to an occasional writer for the more serious Press.

The first is some sort of intuitive insight into what English people in general are thinking and feeling, a glimpse of the national mood of the moment. (It is this, and not any technical devices and skills, that chiefly explains the wide appeal of my war-time broadcasts.) When it is working—and I think it worked in several of these pieces—it enables me to be a jump ahead of the politicians, leader-writers and assorted pundits. The other small advantage I have is that my mind, however it may be rated, is my own; nobody has hired it; no hidden plan of campaign guides it; and what it chiefly desires, even more than applause, is that English people should have a good life.

My warmest thanks go to the editor of the *New Statesman and Nation* both for originally printing all these pieces except the last, (originally delivered as the 1955 Herman Ould Memorial Lecture for the P.E.N.,) and for giving permission to reprint them. At the risk of irritating the reader by occasional repetitions and topical references, I have reprinted the pieces without changing anything. For this, after all, was what I was asked to do, as I said at the beginning.

J.B.P.

THOUGHTS IN THE WILDERNESS

THOUGHTS
IN THE WILDERNESS

Many people who write to me, often in a spirit of ill
will, seem to be under the impression that I have moved
from the Left to the Right. Yet in the only public pronouncement I made on this subject, in an article I was
invited to write for a popular newspaper, I was careful
to begin by pointing out that nothing of this kind had
occurred. I said then: "I have not swung from official
Left to official Right. And the notion that this is the
only possible movement seems to me the great fallacy of
our time."

There was, of course, a certain article of mine in a
notorious special issue of *Collier's*. This produced a fine
crop of angry letters, not one of which dealt with the article
they attacked me for writing. They should, in fact, have
been addressed to the editor. What I was asked to write—
and what I wrote—was an imaginary piece of cultural
history, in which I tried my hardest to express my sympathy with and admiration for the essential character of
the Russian people. (It was actually praised by some
persons who knew the subject and took the trouble to read
the article.) I expressed no admiration for the Soviet
Government because I have none, believing its policy
since 1945 (when it immediately opened fire on our
Labour Government) to be monstrously ill-advised. But

I

my own contribution to that *Collier's* issue was anything but brash American propaganda.

Nor am I any nearer the Conservative Central Office than I was early in 1951, when abuse from its admirers arrived at my house in sack loads. I am as much out with the Right (and can prove it, too) as I have always been. Only now I am also out with the Left. This leaves me in a political wilderness. For some time I felt sad about this exile, but then I discovered that many other people, if they had no vested interest in politics as they are, were really in the wilderness with me. Even some of the men with the vested interest would, if pressed, admit that there is a wilderness atmosphere just now, with little that appears to be blossoming and fruitful. I noticed the other week that that experienced and enthusiastic political journalist, Mr. A. J. Cummings, had had to confess, on returning from his holiday, that nobody seemed to be talking politics. And is that because people feel that at last our political, economic, social problems are solving themselves? It is not.

Polemics and theory—and I have tried to take fair samples of them—do not seem to me any more exciting and promising than recent political practice. Even when arriving from the further Left, presumably nourished by passionate ambition or hopeful youth, these books and pamphlets have had about them an air of staleness. The old phrases were trotted out and round, like ageing circus ponies. No new creative ideas flashed into sight. Nothing arrived from an unfamiliar direction. Not a glimmer of insight was revealed. The mind received never a jolt. The writers were not foolish, they were often sensible and clearly aware of our plights; but they seemed to be nearly as bored as we were. Still keeping to the Left side, we can say that nothing could be more wearily different from the thrust of ideas, the eager debates, the electric clashes (State Socialism, Guild Socialism, Syndicalism) of the decade thirty to forty years ago, than this routine yawning parade of opinions, as if everybody were dressed in black coat and striped trousers and dreadfully short of sleep.

The economists, too, give me the impression of men who have toiled too long in fields that are exhausted. I am not capable of deciding between them, but I am fairly certain that not one of them could produce in me enough energy to dig up a basketful of potatoes. They may reasonably retort that it is not their business to give us energy. Nevertheless, in effect they are always telling us we need more, that we must behave better—or else! And the truth is that, however much we may need their advice, we are tired of them. They fail to arouse our enthusiasm, they can no longer even capture our interest, because what they give us we do not want and what we probably want they cannot give us. The soil in which they work is exhausted, infertile; we seem to need a few fields that have been lying fallow.

It seems to me that people in general are aware, if only obscurely, of this central vacuum. Because people spend their evenings watching idiotic parlour games on TV or *Chu Chin Chow* on ice, this does not mean that the last glimmer of intuitive perception has been dowsed, though after a few more years of mass communication on this level the crowd may be permanently half-witted. But now, I think, they are still aware of something missing. And this,

I fancy, explains the perfervid atmosphere of the Corona-
tion and the Test Matches, the hopeless overdoing of anything likely to waken the crowd. We are a political people
without any real politics. We are moral campaigners
without a campaign.

If I say that we seem to have gone as far as we can with
our present set of political-economic ideas and machinery,
that we need an approach from a new direction, that some
creative overmastering idea should find its way to the
hollow centre, some old hands will tell me I am encouraging some pseudo-mystical nonsense that will end up as
Fascism. In my own case I think not. Fascism implies the
State in all its power and majesty; and, like many people
now out in the wilderness, I distrust the State. (Even as a
Left propagandist I never advocated State collectivism.)
It is one of our grievances against the two big political
parties, now playing Box and Cox for us, that they are
both State parties, even though one of them pretends not
to be. Outside the wilderness it is thought laughable that
any party should seriously challenge the State; yet nobody
in his senses laughs at what are plainly the results of our
subservience to the idea of the State.

There is much to be said for the view that the citizen of
any contemporary great Power is the biggest donkey of all
time. He is not himself aggressive, and instead of yelling
for war, as his forefathers sometimes did, he loathes the
very thought of it. Yet he denies himself more and more,
sacrifices more and more, to this war-making instrument,
the State, which behaves as if it were the creation of some
demi-urge who hated our whole species. Of course we do
it, because 'they' do it. But then 'they' do it, because we

4

do it. And if we took power away from the State, which alone makes war, instead of giving it more and more, often at the sacrifice of most of the arts and graces of life, then none of us would do it.

More and more I for one mistrust that bigness before which a man feels helpless and baffled. Once past a sensible size, things get out of hand, acquiring an alien sinister life of their own, apt to prey upon our humanity. Men who work for vast organisations begin to lose sight of their original purpose. Very soon, more and more authority is given to tidy cold-blooded administrative types, and fewer and fewer opportunities are given to untidy hot-blooded creative types. The rebel, if he is not forcibly silenced, is almost muzzled by being denied the huge and expensive channels of communication. (What are your chances of running a national newspaper, a film studio and chain of cinemas, a TV network?) And this bigness, because of its size and complexity, encourages us to forget that our communal life is entirely our own creation, that if we do not like the forms it has adopted we can change them.

After all, there is one rough-and-ready test, which among all the fuss and bullying we may not remember. For what matters is what is happening in people's minds, the quality of the experience there; and this is all that matters. The objective-material view will not do at all. If a city is miraculously efficient, crammed with goods, bristling with services, glittering with all the latest ingenuities, but is also filled with people who are worrying themselves sick, or becoming ugly-minded and cruel, or turning into dim robots, then that city is a flop. If the

5   B

people in the neighbouring country are comparatively poor, have few possessions, no gadgets, no great organisations, but contrive to live zestfully, laugh and love, still enjoy poetry and music and talk, then that country has succeeded. It is, I repeat, a rough-and-ready test, only certain for ourselves; but I feel we cannot start applying it too soon, using it aggressively against the power-maniacs, the society-my-guinea-pig scientists, the inventors-at-any-cost, the sales-and-advertising men, the officials-who-are-more-important-than-we-are.

This attitude of mind will find no more genuine support on the Left than it will on the Right. But before returning to the wilderness—or, as some witty Honourable Member might suggest, to the green room—I will scatter a few queries. For example, friends. Do you feel about the English in general what you did ten years ago—honestly now? What relation to their work have the happiest men you know? Women and children need security but do men, real men? ("He insisted upon security for himself" would be an odd opening of a biography.) Which of your boards and committees delight in original, creative-minded men? How many persons whom you respect prefer minimum hours of work and plenty of passive amusement to the chance of working like blazes making something? Which is winning—mass communication or education? Is our society becoming more flexible or less—and if you think 'more', have you tried starting anything good lately? Are there more rich, fiery, independent characters about? Are men's deepest needs being increasingly satisfied? And if you reply that they are not *just now*, will you explain how the promised land is to be reached by way of two vicious

6

circles, one of frustration, rage, and violence, the other of apathy, triviality, and exhaustion? Can any sensible plan succeed if there is a cold dying centre? Do we want more and more Left (plus, in the end, more police), more and more Right (more police again), or something that is neither, inspired by fresh thinking?

Yes, I will close the door quietly.

MASS
COMMUNICATIONS

Mr. Edward Hyams has told me that a hundred thousand people buy my books and millions read them. I am sorry, but he is out of date, well behind the times. The books now that are bought and read on this scale are no longer written by professional authors but by young men who have been sailing rafts or getting themselves lost in the jungle. I noticed the other day in a local bookshop that all the books most prominently displayed were of this sort. This is the trend, as any bookseller or 'literary' editor will tell you. The status of the man of letters is sharply declining. It may be true, as we are often told, that we have neither the talent nor the personality of the old masters of authorship, the men I admired in my youth; but that is not the whole story. The truth is, we live in quite a different world.

When I was young, before the First War, some of the best prose of the time appeared in morning papers. Moreover, even the most popular of these papers devoted a fair amount of space to the pronouncements, debates, quarrels, of men like Shaw, Wells, Chesterton, Belloc. Shaw especially owed much of this constant reporting to the figure he cut in the public eye. Who receives this kind of attention now? The answer, of course, is Mr. Gilbert Harding. And I know Mr. Harding sufficiently well to declare confidently that he does not think of himself as another Shaw, Wells, or Chesterton. He happens to be a frequent and effective performer on radio and TV. But that is enough, for now we are in a different world, in which we are already within sight of what might be called the Pay-off of Mass Communications.

Now if Mr. Hyams had told me to stop writing books in the wilderness and to make use of mass communications, he would at least have been bang up to the minute. For it is there that you will find the attentive and admiring millions. And it happens that I have one of those rough-and-tumble personalities that are effective in these media, being far removed from the sensitive plants that wither when all the lights are switched on. I know most of the tricks of popular journalism, film, radio, TV. But, unfortunately, I regard these things with suspicion and growing alarm. They are busy creating a world I dislike intensely. Now it would be a sweet gag to use mass communications in order to denounce them—like that admirable headmaster who advised his TV audience to sell their sets and buy a good edition of Plato—but one's chances of bringing it off regularly are very small indeed. Any advice on this matter, sent privately and, preferably, typewritten, will be gratefully received.

As a matter of fact, I had an honest shot at it only the other week, when I asked my agent to see the managing editor of one of our most popular dailies on my behalf. I wanted, I told him, to write a series of brief, pungent articles entitled 'Unpopular Opinions' in which, instead of flattering their customers, I would challenge most of their values and assumptions. But these wily fellows were not having any. They pointed out that their circulation was steadily rising and that, in effect, they did not propose to check it by disturbing their readers. Nor could I blame them. To succeed in mass communications you must flatter the customer and never disturb him. And that, of course, is what is happening, on a gigantic scale in America, and on an increasing scale here and elsewhere. So we spend billions on education, only to have the good work—if it is good work—rapidly undone by the mass communication experts, waiting to pounce on the boys and girls as they come out of school.

Thousands and thousands of extremely clever men and women are now engaged not (to use the old, forgotten phrase) in the task of 'elevating the masses' but in the business of catering to all their whims, prejudices, and idiocies. All day and half the night there are conferences in newspaper and magazine offices, film, radio and TV studios, deciding how everything can be shaped, coloured, cut down and trimmed, to flatter and tickle the mob of customers. If 'they' like this, it is in; if 'they' don't like that, it is out. Everything must be made smooth and easy. No effort must be required. History must be falsified, science distorted, religion sentimentalised, human relations hopelessly over-simplified, so that nobody is challenged, disturbed, asked to reflect or feel deeply. It is a kind of nursing-home view of entertainment. The bedside manner, formerly used only for rich, foolish old women, is now laid on for millions. And as we approach the Pay-off, the patron is asked to do less and less. He need not leave his fireside, stir from his chair. His children, lured away from books, need no longer create visual images, for these will be supplied with the TV set. Even his parlour games will be played for him, so that he need no longer trouble to know his neighbours. Even TV politics are just round the corner, and, indeed, when I was in America a year ago, they seemed to have already arrived. The lazy half-wit, once a despised character except on fair grounds and at election times, has at last come into his own.

Younger readers must accept my assurance that all this is new. Fifty years ago there was little of this mass catering. Even a popular newspaper was rather better than its average reader, who was expected to make some effort. Even the music-hall offered flashes of genuine art and genius, to please a Max Beerbohm. There was no elaborately organised and publicised mass culture. Ordinary people were supposed to tag along somewhere on the fringes of real culture. The representatives of that culture may not have been widely appreciated but they existed as public figures, vaguely revered if not thoroughly understood, and had not then been driven out of sight and mind by the blown-up personalities of mass communication. Young people could easily pass from popular nonsense to an enjoyment of fine work, for there it was, waiting for them, and they were not deliberately herded away from it, kept by sinister magic in a closed circle of false mass culture, which is what is happening now. Unluckily, too, this circle was more or less completed at a time when large numbers of people suddenly found themselves with more money to spend and more leisure. This partly explains the failure of the promise of the war years, when many of us were far too optimistic. We did not realise then how easily mass culture, with its immense resources of publicity, could defeat us. We were like a man with a woodcut trying to compete with a four-colour poster thirty feet by ten.

Though I must have spent as much time with books, music, pictures as any man my age, I am sometimes represented to be an enemy of the arts, chiefly, I imagine, because I have occasionally laughed at pretentious æsthetes. But it is another of my grievances against mass culture that its existence shapes and encourages anti-mass culture, which seems to me thin, sterile, and often false. Thus, in B.B.C. terms, the Third Programme is as bad in its way as the Light Programme. It contains too much that is merely pretentious, amateurish, and debilitated. If I do not want Irving Berlin on a cinema organ, neither do I want coldly pedantic suites scored for harsh strings and an acid woodwind. Third-rate comics are unsatisfactory, but then so too are third-rate professors who have never learnt how to talk on the air. Thrillers written in American slang are sad bosh, and so are 'experimental' novels, without narrative and characters, served up in dollops of bogus poetic prose: what is missing from both is talent. If mass communications belong too exclusively to the market-place, the culture that deliberately reacts against it is often too far away from the market-place. Too many people who rebel against mass culture imagine now that genuine 'Art' must be identified with extreme introversion. It is taken for granted that the extroverted attitude belongs to entertainers or charlatans. Much of our recent criticism seems to have been written by disappointed men about invalids. The arts are so precious, fancy, and fenced-off that ordinary sensible men and women begin to despair of enjoying them, giving them up as a bad job. And all this self-conscious attitudinising, all these elaborate antics, are not part of a direct response to life itself but have been produced by the deliberate reaction against mass standards. They are in fact a by-product of mass communications.

A final fact, sadly unnoticed, about mass communications is that they are parasitic upon the very things they are trying to kill. They borrow and ruin talent, hardly ever create it. Thus it is the Theatre that trains playwrights, directors, actors, and not TV, which merely seduces the Theatre's patrons. It is the old-fashioned publisher or editor who discovers new writers and often keeps them alive. After twenty-five years of radio, and all the fuss there has been about it, only the feeblest glimmer of genuine new talent has ever been detected. The film studios and the popular Press scream at us about wide screens and 3D and the rest of it, when all that is required are good stories, sensitive acting, some genuine communication to us. The machinery comes first; the human factor, the blessing of talent, a long way after. It is typical of this new age that a man pays twelve shillings a week for a TV set and only sixpence for all that comes out of it. Meanwhile, the true old magic, which depends upon real communication between devoted men and women of shining talent and audiences willing to make an effort, is rapidly fading. Soon the machinery will be perfect, but all entrancing experience gone and forgotten. Perhaps the world will be run by robots; but nobody will notice the difference.

BLOCK THINKING

My children being too old for such things, my grand-children still too young, I do not know if they still exist; but there used to be offered in the toyshops sheets of card-board to which were fixed the miniature outfits of bus conductors, soldiers, cowboys, and so forth. A small boy presented with one of these outfits could at once transform himself, to his own deep satisfaction, into the fascinating figure of his daydreams. All you had to do was put on the hat, take the gun, the whistle, the badge: there you were, completely outfitted.

Now it seems to me that during the last twenty years there has been a great deal of this Complete Outfitting far away from toyshops, in the world of our beliefs and opinions. It might also be called Block Thinking. Neat sets of beliefs and opinions are fastened together; and you are expected to take the lot. Either live in one Block or go and find a room in the next Block. Stay in the street out-side, and you will be sniped at from all the windows. A Completely Outfitted man, a good Block Thinker, would rather have a fellow from the other Block, properly Outfitted, than tolerate a ditherer without a Block and Outfit. Let him shuffle off to the wilderness where he belongs!

I remember the hours I spent in the 'thirties arguing with people who thought they were much cleverer than I was. (I am not very clever, but a bit cleverer than I look, like many seemingly gormless West Riding men.) They would try to prove to me that I had no choice except between Fascism and Communism. Your money or your life? Black or Red? So they were joining the C.P.; and most of them since have written long articles and books— and not done badly out of them—explaining that when they were Communists they were not really Communists. It all seems sadly out of date now, of course, but the attitude of mind is still with us, the Blocks and Outfits still in fashion. Probably the same people, grown no wiser, have the same contempt for my lack of insight and decision now that they had then. What Block are you in? Where is your Outfit? Bah!

Let us say, for example, that you believe that when the men responsible for atom bombs and other horrors solemnly warn their audiences, composed of people who never asked for any of this, that they live in a perilous age, those audiences should throw their chairs at the platform, to show what they think of such impudence. Write something to this effect, perhaps omitting the chair-throwing but making your protest, and immediately messages arrive from the Pacifist Block, telling you that you only need more courage and consistency to be entitled to wear the Outfit. Yet you may be anything but a turner of cheeks. You may believe in the most murderous direct defence of your own homes and persons, with pistols and lead pipes for men, sharp knives for the girls, holding that if the other fellows do not want to be killed, they should not obey orders to leave their own homes and ruin other people's. You may believe, as I do, that if the citizens of Great

Powers were more sharply militant, less like sheep, then States would soon be less like wolves.

Again, your attitude towards Science may be ambivalent, as mine is. You may be profoundly sceptical about scientific humanism and its air-conditioned cybernetics utopia round the corner. You may feel that pseudo-scientific thought about man and the universe, sinking into the popular mind, has done much to create a mood of despair, making men feel homeless exiles, caught in a blind machine. You may take a sour view of recent contributions of nuclear physics to human progress, and discover in its professors a certain irresponsibility. But if you say these things in print, there arrives a triumphant messenger from the Catholic Block, crying: "What did we tell you? Now admit, you are one of us." Whereas you may be not one of them at all, may feel entitled to be as sceptical about the Pope and the priests as you are about the British Association. A man may think that scientists should make narrower claims and take longer-term views and yet not want to climb on to the Angst-wagon of Original Sin and Guilt and Sex-lit-with-Hellfire.

This brings a loud cheer from the Rationalist Block. But it does not follow that you can join it. The accommodation it offers may seem much too small. For though you may not believe, with the Black gang, that man reached his noblest height in the thirteenth century and that the Renaissance was a blot on our history, you may yet hold that men need some form of religion, and that it is our misfortune if we find ourselves without one, among a litter of symbols that have lost their magic. You may know, as I do, men and women who never enter a church to worship there, yet seem more deeply possessed by genuine religious feeling than most of the ecclesiastical propagandists, hell-fire novelists, cold and cautious advocates of a Christian Society without faith, hope, or charity.

It is true that if a writer does not belong to a Block, goes about without a Complete Outfit, he suffers from many disadvantages. He has to think for himself, and thus may appear slow-witted as well as vague and 'woolly'. (You are always 'woolly' if you have no Outfit.) He has no access to a Block list of witty retorts and crushing counter-arguments. He may still be groping and fumbling about while his Outfitted opponent has whipped out the cowboy gun, the bus-conductor's bell, the policeman's whiste. A sound Block man has more respect for a fellow from the opposite Block than he has for woolly ditherers, and nine times out of ten would rather leave one Block for another than stay outside in the rain. Once they have worn a Complete Outfit, most men feel naked without one.

What is most important, however, is that a writer solidly established in a Block can count on its support. At a time when critical standards are uncertain, when independent judgment is fast disappearing, when the prizes are few and so increasingly valuable, this Block support is almost worth a goldmine. Thus, there are some æsthetic enterprises that are hardly likely to succeed without some assistance from the Inverts' Block—called by a sardonic friend of mine 'the Girls' Friendly Society'—which enthusiastically gives its praise and patronage to whatever is decorative, 'amusing', 'good theatre', witty in the right way, and likely to make heterosexual relationships look ridiculous: all of which is probably the stiff price we are paying in London for our stupid laws against inversion.

Clearly nothing can be achieved in politics without a Block. Even those of us who mistrust Block thinking, Complete Outfits on cards, would have to form some sort of Block to assert our essential liberalism. (Though guerrillas have been known to succeed against regular armies.) Where I disagree with many of my correspondents is in believing that a man is not necessarily useless just because he remains outside the Blocks. Many of us feel that this is a time when it is better to be 'woolly' than Completely Outfitted. For men are in despair. Most people who join the Blocks, accepting with relief some ready-made system, do it out of despair. That is why they are so often angry and intolerant, having arrived at their decision not by way of hope and love but through despair and terror. You can smell all this in the very air of our time: we seem to live among savage rats and screaming mice. We are in despair because we begin to feel that our problems are beyond our solution, our dilemmas intolerable. But the worst way out of this situation may be to hurry to the nearest Block and to man the guns there. This will settle nothing except perhaps the hash of Western Man.

We must think, and think in a fresh, creative fashion. One glimmering of a new idea, in our situation, is worth all the blaze and fury of the Block systems, with their propaganda and anathemas. For, as possible solutions, not as power systems, they are all out of date. The Outfit is Complete just because it is done with. Every Block known to me is old-fashioned, like all fortresses. Every man who joins one, proudly accepting its logic and consistency, has really stopped trying to shape the future. It is he, and not the vague woollies outside, who has given it up as a hopeless job. For example, what is the world's Number One Problem? Not one Block will give the right answer. Yet there it is glaring at us: "What can we do now that will prevent our great-grandchildren from eating one another?" But perhaps here I do some of the Block systems an injustice; for at least they are working hard to prevent our having any great-grandchildren.

Our remote ancestors, we are told, were not impressive creatures, they cut a poor figure among the great beasts of the forest; they had no huge claws and teeth, no scaly armour, no wings, no great turn of speed, not even the power of rapid reproduction: all the odds seemed heavily against them. But they had one miraculous trick—they could adapt themselves to make the best of changing conditions; they were flexible and experimental. And now that we have conquered—and nearly ruined—the earth, now when we ourselves change our conditions often at appalling speed and almost blindly, we are in sore need of all the adaptability our species can still discover in itself. We must think freshly, think fast, improvise, experiment, and be tolerant of one another's mistakes. Despair and hate are not going to help us. And neither, I fancy, is Block thinking.

THEY COME
FROM INNER SPACE

Circling this globe, usually at very high altitudes, are space ships superior to any type of aircraft we have as yet produced. The creatures in these space ships, presumably from another planet (which may not belong to our solar system), are watching us. They are not hostile, try to avoid any clash with our aircraft, but will not allow any close investigation, and if necessary will wreck any persistent pursuer. We may reasonably assume that they are more intelligent than we are, representing a further stage of scientific and mechanical development. We do not know why they are here; perhaps they are merely curious, perhaps they are making plans to take over this planet or to intervene in our affairs. But here they are, watching us, probably through enormous cold eyes that would strike us dead with terror.

So runs the Flying Saucer legend, which has already found its way into all manner of print. It does not come to us from those places where statues drip blood or witches and vampires abound; neither poets nor peasants have contributed to it. We owe the Flying Saucers to airmen, technicians and the like, all members of communities that pride themselves on their realism and common sense. It is hard luck on these fellows, of course. Just as they are beginning to feel that through science, 'technics', and 'know-how' they are masters of life, it seems that little blue monsters arrive from outer space to spy on them, behaving in a fashion that apparently makes them feel inferior and *somehow guilty*. As if our galaxy police had been called in! But the rest of us, who have never seen a Saucer, should not be too surprised. We should remember that no natural movements ever seem to be in a straight line but always take us a circular or spiral way. So if we leave all the old nonsense behind, run as fast as we can away from gods and devils, saints and witches, we only arrive at the place where three-headed Martians are watching us. In short, the old wild dreams of the Unconscious break through. Moved by feelings we refuse to recognise, we project uncanny and sinister images against the very sky itself. What secret bitterness is in the Cup to which these are the Saucers?

During recent visits to America I have read a good deal of science fiction, which is now produced over there in astonishing quantities, both in magazine and volume form. (There is more and more of it here too, and a fair amount, I noticed some weeks ago, in Western Germany and Switzerland.) I am no authority on this stuff, but I have sampled enough of it to be able to criticise it without injustice. Roughly it can be divided into three kinds. The first is bosh consisting of corny short stories, on the gangster or Western pattern, with a few rocket ships, atomising pistols, and mysterious planets thrown in; they are essentially no different from the stories we used to read about Chicago, Dawson City, and Tombstone, Arizona. If such hack work could arouse thought, then we should think what a pity it is that our idiotic species is shortly proposing to spread its dreary melodramatic doings from here to

C

Sirius. But no thought comes. This is trade rubbish, like the beads and Brummagem gauds that the nineteenth-century traders took with them into the jungle. We can forget this kind, though its specimens must far outnumber the rest.

The second type has not much more literary merit but is more original. It seems to be chiefly written by men (I have yet to notice a woman in this field) who have at least a smattering of scientific and technical knowledge and a vast enthusiasm for inventions and gadgets. They are the same men who write articles telling us how fortunate we are to be living in this age of scientific marvels, and how in the near future we shall find ourselves in a wonderland of labour-saving devices, surrounded by attentive robots. They are the cybernetics public relations team. (Perhaps some of them are already robots.) So their stories of the year 2027 and 2148 are crammed with the most astonishing devices, with everybody living a push-button life on this and various other planets. But these enthusiasts cannot communicate their enthusiasm in such stories. Indeed, an air of boredom creeps in. Their plastic, electronic, atomic-power-run cities seem to be inhabited by stale ghosts. Rocket ships are flashing millions of miles from one tower of tedium to another. Even inter-planetary wars or a police pursuit that covers half the Milky Way bring little zest. The robots, now all over the place, are having the best of it. If, as it appears at times, they are about to take over, nothing will be lost.

The third kind, still sparsely represented, differs from the other two in being genuinely imaginative and having some literary merit. One of its authors, whose work can be sampled here, is Mr. Ray Bradbury. His stories use the familiar properties of science fiction—fabulous travel in space and time, wars between planets, weird beings from beyond the solar system—but not in the usual routine fashion. He is concerned not with gadgets but with men's feelings. He creates imaginatively; and it may be assumed that he is not merely turning out stuff for a new and flourishing market but is trying to express some of his own deepest feelings. It is significant that he lives in Southern California, that advance post of our civilisation, with its huge aircraft factories, TV and film studios, automobile way of life (you can eat and drink, watch films, make love, without ever getting out of your car), its flavourless cosmopolitanism, its charlatan philosophies and bogus religions, its lack of anything old and well-tried, rooted in tradition and character. Here, on this sign-post to the Future, sits Mr. Bradbury, telling us his dreams.

They are very sinister. When they impose themselves on us, they fill us with a sense of desolation and horror. Compared with these glimpses of the future, most of the old hells seem companionable and cosy. This is a world, we feel, to get out of soon as we can. An excellent covering title for these tales of tomorrow would be *Better Dead*. The price our descendants will pay for our present idiocies is terrible. After us—not the deluge but the universal nightmare. One of Mr. Bradbury's favourite devices, not without its symbolism, is the sudden transformation of the familiar and friendly into something appallingly menacing, so that just when you think all is well, you are trapped—these are not the people who will help your time-travelling escape but the police from the nightmare future; this is not

23

your long-lost brother but a Martian who has assumed his appearance. The physicist, the astronomer, the biologist, may smile at the liberties such fantasies take, or dismiss their obvious improbabilities with a shrug. But can we afford those smiles and shrugs? I think not.

Science fiction and Flying Saucer legends seem to me important because they show us what is really happening in men's minds. Like the sexually sadistic thrillers now so popular, they are the myths and characteristic dreams of our age, and are psychologically far more important than our more rational accounts of ourselves. They take the lid off. They allow us a glimpse of what is boiling down below. They may be the first rumblings of the volcano that will overwhelm us. Of course our political leaders, solemn experts, pundits of platform and Press, do not concern themselves with such trivialities, for they still imagine, against all the evidence, that men are as rational as they like to think they are, are moved by a limited set of obvious motives, and consciously direct their affairs. And to imagine this is as sensible and safe as it is to assume that what can be seen of an iceberg is all there is of it. If we are all in the same boat, then its name is *Titanic*.

Behind all these topical tales, fables and legends, it seems to me, are deep feelings of anxiety, fear, and guilt. The Unconscious is protesting against the cheap conceit and false optimism of the conscious mind. Having ruined this planet, we take destruction to other planets. This very extension in space of our activities is desolating, at least to minds that are not entirely childish, because it is a move, undertaken in secret despair, in the wrong direction. We have to go somewhere, so we prefer superficially to think of ourselves travelling to the other side of the sun rather than sitting quietly at home and then moving inward, exploring ourselves, the hidden life of the psyche. All this comes of trying to live a dimension short, with infinite length and breadth, from here to Sirius, but with no depth, without the spirit.

The tone and the atmosphere of these new stories are very different from those of the early scientific romances. The spiritual climate has changed. The rocket ships no longer represent man's triumphant progress. They merely show him hurrying at ever-increasing speeds away from his true life as a spiritual being. He is trying to escape from himself. He cannot come to terms either with this good earth or his own soul; he is rootless, destructive, insane, so goes hurtling and screaming, a lost spirit, into endless black space. So uncertain is he now, so fearful, so deeply suspicious, that a ring of friendly faces may be suddenly transformed into dreadful invaders from space, the ultimate strangeness and menace. Alternatively, his dreams are so dark with guilt that any wandering balloon may be seen as a ship from another planet, into which are projected images of creatures wiser and better than we are, no doubt wondering how long we should be allowed to inhabit this earth. The legends may be absurd, the literature trivial; but the stir in the Unconscious that has brought such stuff to the surface, to exercise an uncanny fascination over so many minds, is neither absurd nor trivial. We are being warned.

We are in fact warning ourselves that our society, like a rocket ship bound for some distant nightmare planet, is hurrying at full speed in the wrong direction; and that, dangerously over-extraverted, we are refusing to deal justly with the unconscious side of our minds. In our conceit, we are withholding tribute from the gods, who may appear at any moment in their most terrible guise. We are trying to live outside the dimension of spirit, to close the frontiers of the ancient hidden kingdoms. We have so elevated the masculine principle, so depressed and humiliated the feminine principle, that we can no longer draw sustenance from the earth nor hope for Heaven; we are uprooted, homeless, half-mad with pride and fear; we spawn invading monsters, all jellied eyes and writhing tentacles, in our despairing souls; we are disappointed, angry, destructive, because the juice and the flavour of this life are harder and harder to find, because the magic is fading, and so we are ready to wreck this or any other planet. We ought to try living sensibly on this earth, perhaps under a matriarchy for a few centuries, with all our saucers quietly supporting our tea-cups.

THE HESPERIDES
CONFERENCE

The Hesperides Conference was on the highest level and of exceptional size. Not only were all the leaders of the Great Powers there but also all their Foreign Ministers, Chiefs of Staffs, and top busybodies. Experts on foreign affairs and leading political commentators from America, Russia, Britain, and France descended upon the island, to grumble about the small back bedrooms that had been allotted to them. Articles discussing the possible results of the Conference appeared in the world's Press. They were as usual quite futile but at least provided their writers with a fair living. Highly paid reporters, flown to the island at enormous expense, told their readers, at an overall cost of about ten pounds a word, that the cigars smoked by the British Prime Minister seemed half an inch longer than usual, that the President of the United States was already playing golf, that the members of the Soviet Delegation had been seen eating caviare and drinking vodka. Newsreel men took the usual shots of bigwigs meeting and greeting other bigwigs at the airport. The F.B.I. investigated the salad chef of the Hotel Bristol. The Russians installed two microphones (which did not work) into the smokeroom of the Savoy-Plaza Hotel. A member of the French Delegation plunged into a rapturous affair with a honey-coloured American secretary. An oldish member of the

British Delegation began taking a strong interest in the piano-accordion player at the Beach Café-Bar. Two American correspondents, after four hours of bourbon-on-the-rocks, swung punches at each other and broke twelve glasses. The weather was beautiful. The Conference began.

It was during the third morning, when the head of the Russian Delegation was making a speech about everything, that several high-level personages first lost consciousness. As usual there had been plenty of yawns and several men had dropped off, but that was only to be expected. When, however, the session was adjourned for lunch, and the French Foreign Minister, among others, refused to wake up, it was realised that this was no ordinary bout of somnolence. By nightfall, after the British Delegation's cocktail party had been abandoned, all the leaders and Foreign Ministers had succumbed to this mysterious malady and had lost consciousness. Most of the Chiefs of Staffs and junior Ministers and expert advisers crawled to their beds during the following twenty-four hours. On the fifth day, the Hesperides Conference was in a coma.

Lord Ward and Sir Thomas Tittlemouse arrived by special plane from London. Doctors Elmer K. Jefferson and Herman Funf were rushed from Johns Hopkins to the American Delegation. Professor Oskarvitz, from Moscow, and Professor Nicolia, of Erivan, came to look after the Soviet representatives. Paris, Lyons, and Marseilles sent their finest specialists to examine the unconscious French politicians, soldiers, and officials. The games room of the Savoy-Plaza was turned over to the medical men, who began to hold a sort of conference themselves, and once they felt certain that their distinguished patients were in no immediate danger, began to enjoy themselves. The best resources of these hotels were now at their disposal. They were able to compare notes on this and other medical problems. The weather was still beautiful. The young Frenchman and the honey-coloured American secretary were still highly conscious, at least of each other, and had a glorious time.

Most of the foreign affairs experts, who had already begun sketching out articles called *After Hesperides—What?*, were victims of the strange sleeping sickness, remaining motionless in their little back bedrooms, now as good as any other. But the reporters in general had escaped the malady, and now they despatched hundreds of thousands of words to the astonished world, giving the verdicts of the assembled medical men and describing the amazing scene with all the wealth of adjectives at their command. The newsreel men were not allowed to film the unconscious great, but some excellent shots were made of less important victims and it was clearly indicated that if you had seen one you had seen, in effect, the lot. With the result that newsreel theatres in every capital city did wonderful business.

Bulletins were broadcast and published in the Press every few hours during the first days, and then daily after a week or two. There were as many theories as there were doctors on the spot. What was certain, after a week or so, was that nobody was in immediate danger, all pulses and respiration being excellent, that all the victims were in something more than a sound long sleep but in nothing more than a very light coma, and that there seemed no reason why they should not wake up as suddenly as they fell asleep. It was generally agreed too that the older delegates, who had existed under a severe strain for years and had made far too many journeys by plane, would probably benefit from this enforced immobility and lack of consciousness. One theory, indeed, took as its basis the idea that the root cause was mental rather than physical, taking the form of a group regression of libido.

Meanwhile, in all the countries concerned, no new appointments were made to places of power. The highest Offices of State remained vacant. Foreign Ministries, robbed of their most influential and forceful personalities and much of their authority, limited themselves to modest routine work. The various Governments, not feeling themselves competent to deal on a high level with foreign relations, concentrated upon home affairs, and even here tended to act with caution and restraint. The international situation remained as it was when the Hesperides Conference first assembled. And as most of the experts and leading commentators were themselves still unconscious on the island, and editors shrank from asking other writers to occupy their space, the more serious newspapers and periodicals in the chief capitals of the world devoted more and more of their columns to the discussion of non-political subjects, such as the arts, sciences, philosophy, travel, and the relations between men and women. And the discovery of two new fascinating games to be played on TV at once captured the more popular papers of the U.S., Britain, and France. In Russia, the Press, uncertain what line to take on any subject, dwindled until it almost disappeared.

As weeks passed into months, however, and the Hesperides Conference still remained unconscious, it was only in theory that the international situation stayed the same. As the Conference was officially still in progress, and had not yet announced its decisions, no action, no bold pronouncement in foreign affairs, was considered possible. This state of things soon brought about its own changes. For the first time for many years no important speeches were made, denouncing the West from the East, the East from the West. No new crusade against Communism was mentioned. World revolution was placed in cold storage. Neither God nor the historic destiny of mankind was loudly proclaimed an ally. No threats, no jeers, were exchanged. Even Anglo-American and Franco-British relations, being no longer examined and commented on at a high level, now failed to reach any crises. The Press no longer warned its readers that the hour was at hand. No radio talks asked listeners to stand firm.

Millions of people who had been weighed down with feelings of fear, hate, horror, and guilt now found themselves living in a different world. At last they could breathe freely. They began to make sensible long-term plans for the future. Many groups of scientists, freed temporarily from their researches into the possibilities of atomic and biological warfare, ventured, timidly at first but then with growing confidence, to divert their research into harmless and possibly useful channels. Having a chance at last to mind their own business, the countries represented at the Conference began making some effort to improve the conditions of life, to lighten the burdens of their citizens. Diplomats and minor officials, able for the time being to ignore time-old foreign policies that had never brought anything but disaster, often converted the very scenes of recurring crises into friendly meeting-places. As the chief representatives of the power motive were still unconscious, the power motive itself rapidly lost force and momentum. All the machinery of ideological and national propaganda, lacking the guiding hand, fell into disuse, and plans were eagerly made to spend the vast sums of money now saved, chiefly on various amenities that the over-taxed citizens had hitherto been unable to afford. Without Presidents, Prime Ministers, Foreign Secretaries, the Americans, British, and French did not know what was happening to Anglo-American and Franco-British relations; and for the first time for years began to get along quite nicely. There was even talk of temporarily suspending the rules and regulations about visas and passports. The easy freedom of the pre-1914 world was almost in sight.

It was then that a brilliant young pathologist from Barcelona arrived at the Hesperides. He had a theory, which he explained to the assembled doctors. He also had a small supply of a new and very powerful antibiotic, which he begged to be allowed to inject into three or four of the unconscious men. He was certain it would bring them out of their coma. Finally, he was given permission to treat one Chief of Staff, one Under-Secretary for Foreign Affairs, and one economic adviser. Within an hour, all three were not only awake but beginning to make angry speeches or to demand secretaries to attend them so that they could dictate aggressive memos. It was a triumph for the young man from Barcelona, who declared that if he were given the necessary facilities, he could return within two or three weeks with a sufficient supply of his remedy to revivify the whole Conference. As he announced this, through the long corridors where peace and quiet had reigned for many months, loud angry voices were heard. The medical men exchanged long inquiring glances. They were well aware of what had been happening in the world during the time the Conference had slept.

They escorted the young man back to their head-quarters, the former games room of the hotel, securely barred from the Press. They looked thoughtfully at him. They exchanged more dubious glances. *What was their decision?* No prizes are offered for the best replies.

EROS AND LOGOS

There are some people who become impatient and angry if they are confronted by large, loose, wild generalisations. (They can usually tolerate a few of their own: it is yours they object to.) Such people should not read what follows. It is not for them. I must point out, however, that the object of these pieces of mine is to provoke thought and discussion, chiefly by their refusal to treat routine topics in a routine fashion. They do not pretend to be the Word of the Lord, tablets of stone hauled down from the sacred mountain. I am merely trying to arouse the interest of the English-speaking middle class, overworked, worried, and on the edge of the last ditch. So I am capable of using anthropological and other terms that will set me at cross-purposes with some readers. For example: *matriarchy*. What do I mean when I suggest (partly out of devilment) that a matriarchy might save us?

Certainly I do not mean that Cabinet offices, the Judiciary, the Higher Command, the F.B.I., and the T.U.C. should be taken over as soon as possible by bustling, ambitious women. Nor that the images of fat fertility goddesses should be erected jointly by the Ministries of Works and Agriculture. What I am suggesting is that we should begin substituting, in our scheme of life, the values of the feminine principle, Eros, Yin, for those of the masculine principle, Logos, Yang. These are not identical with male and female. I am myself a fairly robust male but I am devoted to Eros rather than to Logos. Much modern literature, as widely different as the novels of Mr. E. M. Forster and D. H. Lawrence, is a defence of Eros against Logos. On the other hand, many women, including the most aggressive feminists, are devotees of Logos, Yang girls. Not long ago I received a report of a women's conference in which the conclusions, which gave the impression that a woman was simply a neater, kinder sort of man, had clearly been arrived at under the spell of Logos. Those good ladies had not invited Yin to their conference: they probably knew she would not have behaved herself.

Risking the largest and wildest generalisations, let us consider the four Great Powers, America, Russia, Britain, and France, in terms of Eros and Logos, Yin and Yang. It is among the ironies of our time that the two main contestants, America and Russia, both represent societies that have too much Logos and not enough Eros. The rest of us have to choose not between Yin and Yang but between two Yangs. Which is yet another reason why we feel so uneasy, war or no war. We suspect that, whatever happens, Eros is out, not Yang.

Thus I cannot agree with my correspondent who declared that America is a matriarchy. Appearances there are deceptive. Girls may be made much of, there may be much sentiment about Mother, woman (being widowed early) may own much of the wealth of the country, yet American society does not show us Eros triumphant. Its chief values are masculine values. The restlessness, ruthless ambition, emphasis on change, inventions, gadgets, mechanical progress, rather pedantic idealism, the idolatry of business, are all masculine, Yang stuff. That famous phrase "The business of America is *business*" would seem to Eros the manifesto of a lunatic. Even the jazzing up of sex —the girl as 'quite a dish'—is Yang at work. (In the world of Eros it is the mature woman and not the young girl who is important.) Fifth Avenue shows us Logos bribing Eros with silks and gems. Woman in urban America has everything except the deep and lasting rewards of Eros. I once saw a party of middle-aged American women, lined, nervous, haunted, being shown a group of Indian squaws, smiling, fat, sleek as seals. The white women, encouraged by the woman guide, were pitying the red women, who had to do so much of the hard work. But the red women were not pitying themselves: they lived under Eros, and kept on smiling, with just a hint of feminine insolence. Of course, they would have liked to have had washing machines and four sets of nylon underclothes. But not at the Logos price, thank you. Hard work or no hard work, they were living in the right world.

Eros has to come in somewhere, of course, but if the masculine principle is supremely triumphant, not properly balanced, then Eros arrives in an inferior form. The result is a taste for crude sex and hard liquor, sex without personal relationship, drink as a short cut to unconsciousness. Naturally there are a great many Americans who dislike this style of life, but nobody who knows urban America and the literature (often very powerful) that represents it could deny that it is a style of life much in favour there. Eros throws the party when the serious work of the day has been done. When the Yang is tired, he 'phones for the Yin.

But the masculine values are the real values, shaping and colouring society.

The essential Russian character, as displayed by its great literature and even by Party members after ten glasses of vodka in a room without microphones, belongs more to Eros than to Logos, though it has always been haunted by a kind of wild Logos spectre. (Those country houses in Turgenev shows us both the Eros values and the Logos speculation.) But Russian Communism is Logos gone mad. Revolutions nearly always start in an Eros atmosphere, with much talk of private happiness, much love-making and the swearing of eternal friendships, and then soon swing over to Logos, with more laws, more police, more demands for instant obedience. A State that ignores the claims, which ought to be primary, of lovers, husbands and wives, parents and children, represents the Logos at work without any check from Eros. It destroys private happiness, all those relationships and styles of life that are at the heart of Eros, for the sake of a theory, or mere power, or some vague dream of happiness that has never been realised yet. To Eros this is the substance being destroyed for the shadow, and therefore sheer lunacy. If Russia is not a complete hell on earth, that is because Eros, the Yin values, still keep breaking through, though their activities are never on the agenda.

Here, to keep the balance, I must add my belief that a society entirely dominated by Eros would sink into stagnation and sloth, and oddly enough, I suspect, would begin to develop its own cruelties, Yin being as cruel in her way as Yang can be in his. But we need not worry about this state of things. Our immediate dangers are far on the

37

other side. The Yang has his foot pressed down on the accelerator.

We are between two vast and powerful societies that are governed, each in its own way, by the masculine principle not reasonably balanced by the feminine. That such societies should be piling up atom bombs should surprise nobody. This is Logos on the spree. And it is significant that in both these societies the emphasis is on quantities of things rather than on the quality of personal experience. Soviet propaganda and American advertisements often seem to speak with almost the same voice: the management is different but the enterprise is broadly the same. If I must choose, I would prefer an American victory to a Russian one, just as I would prefer writing TV advertisements for Cornflakes to lumbering on thin cabbage soup in Siberia. But I do not want either of these Yang-heavy societies, which are less harmonious, less civilised, less capable of providing the deeper satisfactions, than the smaller and older communities they are dominating and then swallowing. We should have formed a neutral block, wearing the colours of the Yin, under the banner of Eros, who has not yet been completely banished from Western Europe.

Some people see in the Welfare State the handiwork of Eros. I wish I could agree with them. But though Welfare may belong to Eros, the State does not; and it seems to me that in the Welfare State the emphasis is on the State, with Logos firmly in command. (And I cannot help wondering if some of the results of the Welfare State do not show the re-entry of Eros in an inferior form, creating a dim passivity.) There is, however, in British life still a suggestion that Yin is with us. We find traces of her in the flexibility of our official machinery, in our lingering respect for private life, in a traditional piety towards earth, in the wealth of our odd hobbies and pastimes, in the wide network (to which we should cling) of our voluntary associations. Eros still broods over much of our country life.

If we want to see more of Eros, we should look across the Channel. Much of the condemnation of the French comes from the irritation felt by Logos for Eros. Try as they might to meet the Yang commitments, the French cannot help being guided by Yin values. That is why even the people who are most irritated by France, when they are discussing politics, want to spend their holidays there. They need the refreshment, the healing touch, of Eros. They want at least a little time away from the arid lunacies of Logos. And if I were a Frenchman, instead of being apologetic I would rise up in wrathful defence of my country's failure to turn itself into an efficient machine. I would declare that in our apparent Yin chaos, our wild Eros individualism, we were cherishing values that the other Great Powers were beginning to forget; that we were trying to preserve the sensible human scale; that we refused to sacrifice private happiness, discovered in the family, among lovers and friends, in the arts and genuine craftsmanship, for public bosh, power, and statistics; that we still knew, if other people had forgotten, what deep satisfaction came from the service of Eros and the Yin. There are of course many things wrong with France, just as there are with the other three countries, but you can still find there a zest and a sparkle hard to discover in New York, Moscow, or London. It is the twinkle in the eyes of Eros.

39

TIME, PLEASE!

When I was a boy in the North, some of our neighbours, fathers of families, solid taxpayers, had a trick of disappearing now and again from domesticity and respectability, going off on some vast, mysterious binge, from which they returned, after many days, muddy, unshaven, and broke. The type, which must have had a few drops of wild blood that had to be assuaged, has probably vanished for ever now. But I am myself the victim of a similar habit, for every few years I feel compelled to vanish into the mazes of the Time problem, returning, rather worn, with a play or a story. There seems to me—and of course I cannot prove it—no particular emotional drive behind all this. I enjoyed a fairly happy youth and liked pre-1914 England (and think little of the 'twenties that are now coming in for so much praise), but am never conscious of being overwhelmed by any longing for that period of my life. My interest in the Time riddle is part intellectual, part intuitive. I am intellectually curious, like a man faced with some half-deciphered hieroglyphics, and am pricked on, as such a man might be, by an intuitive feeling that here is the great challenge. So a most inadequate Childe Roland returns to the Dark Tower.

The result, whether offered in playhouses or bookshops, is always the same. The public is at once divided into two sharply opposed groups. The first—bless it—consists of people who are as fascinated as I am, and often write letters to tell me so. Some of them, no doubt, are just romantic, tender-minded chumps, but many others are sufficiently tough-minded and may grapple with the problem, in the abstract, with more skill than I can muster. Dunne himself, whom I knew well, could hardly be dismissed as a vague theosophical dreamer, being in fact a hard-headed engineer and mathematician. (And here let me add that time-theories neither begin nor end with Dunne). The opposing group is made up of people, some of them old friends, who are immediately irritated and antagonised by any reference to this problem. They behave at once as if I were asking very awkward and tactless questions, perhaps about a ne'er-do-well brother, a runaway daughter; as if I were unlocking the cupboard hiding the skeleton. If they are critics, they pooh-pooh the whole silly business, often giving the impression that they themselves once went into the thing, on a much higher level, found nothing in it, and are surprised that I am still poking about down there. Not that I begrudge them their bogus air of superiority; it is one of the tricks of the trade; I have often, in other matters, worked it myself. But the general attitude of this group is very curious: I think there is fear lurking somewhere behind it. For heaven's sake, leave that clock alone!

Now it has never been suggested, I think, by any of us time-theorists that a little fiddling with the clock will put all right for us. We have never suggested that there is an easy way out. It is in fact precisely this view that we challenge. What is it people believe now? Some believe that once their souls have sought forgiveness and received grace, the fields of Paradise await them, any monotony being broken by the spectacle of other souls, with whom they may have lunched for years, suffering everlasting torment. Others, ranging from Madras to Los Angeles, believe that their souls visit this world many times, with varying destinies according to the progress they are making. This is not a belief I share, but it does seem rather more reasonable than the one-shot-in-the-dark idea of the universe. Others again, with whom I have more sympathy, tend to see life in terms of various levels of being, and incline to the view that just as the cells of our bodies contribute to and share to some extent in our lives, we in turn contribute to and share in the life of some mysterious world being, an *anima mundi*. And this has at least the advantage of being more or less on the right scale, belonging to a huge and highly complicated universe. Its chief disadvantage is that it seems coldly impersonal, unlikely to hearten us greatly in our struggle to behave decently, to preserve some shreds of honour.

A great many people, however, do not believe any of these things. Life is an accident, they feel, and Man is the best it can do. There is no chain of being in which he might be a link; no God, no gods. The immortal soul belongs to poetry, and poetry is not true. Death cancels out the individual, and sooner or later will blot out the species. The account that science gives us of the universe, though it keeps changing, is the only true one. We all go rolling through black space to our doom. Every tick, every heartbeat, brings us nearer final oblivion. We are fixed in Macbeth's tale told by an idiot. Vanity of vanities!

Now exceptional men may believe all this, and yet contrive to live richly, even nobly, announcing their despair
with ardour and courage. Such men, I suspect, have a
hidden store of idealism, secret hopes; and as a rule it will
be found that they spring from religious stock, have been
nourished in youth by an atmosphere of profound conviction; they might be said to enjoy a heritage, from which
they draw a private income, of decent ethics and reasonable endeavour. Their very rationalism, being positive,
glows with a fervour that is more than rational. They can
enjoy a symbolic life, though they no longer believe in its
symbolism, just because their childhood was shaped and
coloured by it. They will defy the theologians and inquisitors for the sake of the souls they have repudiated. It
is a familiar type, and our history would be a dreary tale
of folly, cowardice and self-seeking without its shining
example. Most of the Liberal Socialists I knew in my
youth were men and women of this sort; and if I complain
too often perhaps it is because I feel that much of what is
happening now is treacherous to their memory. Their
bow of burning gold, their arrows of desire, have been
hidden away in a lumber room; and the Jerusalem we are
building is not Blake's but something horribly like that
place in Palestine.

When masses of men, feeling anything but positive,
come to believe that life is a meaningless accident, that
they are homeless among the cold black spaces, that they
are all huddled together in an execution chamber, that
their humanity is without sense and dignity, then they are
soon trapped within a vicious circle. They allow their
essential rights to be taken away from them. Democracy,

which may be rowdy but is nevertheless based on an idea of man's dignity, becomes a sham. Power is unchallenged; the slave mentality grows. The natural rhythm of work is sacrificed to the machine tempo. The de-humanising process succeeds everywhere. The satisfying patterns of living are broken, and men in the mass, feeling obscurely they have been somehow cheated, burn with resentments that may result finally in mob cruelty. (The signs are with us now.) Above all, this frustrated modern man is haunted by the idea of inexorable passing time. And people who cannot see this are merely keeping their eyes shut tight.

Consider how we are made increasingly aware of time. The coach to Edinburgh left at midday or sunset; the train went at 3.15 or 3.25; the recording of your talk about Edinburgh begins "in ten seconds from now"; and, for all I know, in the labs they may be splitting the seconds. Notice how the best holidays that busy people have are not so much travels in space as escapes into an atmosphere in which the sense of time is easier, the clocks have no seconds hands and perhaps are stopped altogether. And much of the evil of our age comes from the notion that we have merely so much time before oblivion overtakes us. It encourages what I have called elsewhere the cyanide philosophy of life, held by the Nazi leaders, who carried everywhere with them tiny glass ampoules of cyanide so that if the worst came to the worst, they could at once ring down the curtain of death. It has to come down sooner or later, so gamble on doing what the hell you like, while you have time at your disposal, and if you do not succeed —*Curtain!* Which leads automatically to a desire for power at any price, because in the last resort you are not paying the price. You can damn the consequences because in fact you propose to escape the consequences.

But what if, life being not as simple as you imagined it to be, you cannot escape the consequences? What if you can only rid yourself of the world's time, the date on to-morrow's newspaper, but cannot jump out of your own time? Suppose the curtain comes down only between you and the audience and not between you and yourself? It is not my purpose here to discuss time-theories, and I will only point out that there are indeed several of them and that in one form or another they have always haunted the background of man's mind. What interests me here is the effect a rejection of the ordinary time view would have on men's outlook and their conduct. Suppose we began to behave *as if* the time theorist were right. *Leave now for dogs and apes, man has for ever.* Not for ever, perhaps, but a much larger and more complicated portion of time than he generally thinks he had. Which cuts both ways, for now irresponsibility just will not work, and the consequences cannot be escaped. You are stuck with yourself, as people say. If you choose to raise hell, you will live in it.

Here I cannot agree with C. P. Snow, who has said that theories of time appear to him "a mode of denying the seriousness of the moment". On the contrary, I think that such theories encourage a belief in the seriousness of the moment, bringing a creative responsibility, as well as zest, into a man's outlook and conduct. It is slavery to the idea of passing time that at the worst plunges a man into despair and at best merely encourages the view that some-how everything will be better soon. The curious fatalism, almost like a sort of sleep-walking, which is beginning to afflict so many people, making them accept blindly any kind of power-mongering trick, is in my opinion partly the result of this slavery. Once we have said good-bye to eternity, we are well on our way to becoming either devils or robots. But eternity does not mean everlasting time, a misinterpretation that has done much harm. It means non-passing time, another kind of time, existence not measured by clocks and calendars, a level of being that cannot be analysed in any laboratory, belonging to that Kingdom of Heaven which most orthodox Christians refuse to believe is within them, the great Here and Now we enter through the arts and love and friendship and acts of simple goodness; all of which give us the values we must live by, now in danger of being lost. If the reader feels this danger does not exist, then I must withdraw, a timid landlord muttering "Time, please!"

ON EDUCATION

When I was sixteen I left school and found myself a job in a wool office. I had no intention of settling down in the wool business; I had already made up my mind to be a writer, and indeed was already writing hard; but clearly there was no living to be made out of writing for some years to come, so into the office I went. That I was allowed to remain there until I joined the army in 1914 is a tribute to my personality, which then, if not now, was a peculiar mixture of the insufferable and the enchanting; for there cannot have been many young clerks worse than I was in the long history of the wool trade. After about four and a half years in the army I received an ex-officer's grant that took me to Cambridge but by no means kept me there, even on a diet of bread and cheese and boiled eggs, so that I had to eke out with journalism, coaching, odd lectures, anything to earn a guinea or two. Finally, I left Cambridge for London, with some vague introductions and capital of about forty-seven pounds.

Looking back, I can see quite clearly now that the great formative period for me was neither school nor the Cambridge years. It was 1911–14, when nobody was trying to educate me nor paying for me to be instructed, when, in fact, I was working (though as little as possible) in the wool office. Our hours then were longer than most office hours are now: we had to be there at nine, took an hour for

47

lunch, and usually finished sometime between six and seven. (If we worked after seven we received sixpence for tea money. No refreshment was provided before then.) We still sat on high stools like Dickens characters, and I was adroit at looking as if I were entering up the bag book, on my high desk, when in fact I was reading the poems of Yeats or Chesterton's last essays, lying inside my open drawer, which could be closed in a flash. I could also make a slower journey to and from the Bradford Conditioning House, losing myself in daydreams, than anybody else in the trade. Nevertheless, in spite of all these dodges, the office claimed me all the week and never let me go on Saturday until about half-past one. Nor did I live just round the corner from it, for our house, on the edge of the town, was at least two miles away. The fact remains, however, that this was the time when I learnt most and came along fastest. The State was not investing a penny in me.

(And here, for the benefit of those readers who believe in the State but not much in me, let me strike a rough balance. What have I had from the State? A very modest contribution towards my childhood and early youth, a grant that barely kept me alive at Cambridge, and a few fees for jobs undertaken from a sense of duty. What has it had from me? Fortunes in direct and indirect taxation, in Entertainment Tax on my plays and films, in foreign currency it badly needed, to say nothing about my services as a fighting soldier (no great shakes) in one war and as a day-and-night propagandist in another war. And if I should now go broke and dotty, I might receive with luck a Civil List pension of about two hundred a year. That is, if the country can afford it after meeting so many claims upon its generosity. I would have been ten times better off under George the Fourth.)

The truth is, I was fortunate during those years in my environment. My native city of Bradford is frequently mentioned, mostly by people who know nothing about it, as a kind of symbol of 'muck and brass', a stronghold of North-country narrow provincialism. But when I lived there, as a youth, it was considered the most progressive city in the Kingdom. It was a Labour outpost. The first elementary school in the country where meals were provided was the one of which my father was headmaster. We had a Labour weekly to which, during this period, I contributed a regular page. Moreover, a number of Liberal German-Jewish families had settled there, as in Manchester, to give our West Riding dough a leaven of culture. Our Subscription Concerts followed the same plan as those at Leipzig. We also had our Permanent Orchestra and two great Choral Societies. We had three local daily papers as well as several weeklies. We had two theatres and two music-halls. We had a flourishing Arts Club and a Playgoers' Society. Our Central Lending and Reference Libraries were excellent. Bradford men were making their names in the arts and sciences. And though the town was ugly enough, the inviolable moors, where we walked and talked most week-ends, began only a tuppenny tram-ride away. For a few pence more, taking a train, you reached the Dales, the most beautiful countryside in England.

So there we were, walking towards our vast sevenpenny teas, arguing over our pipes of fourpenny Navy Cut, listening to Nikisch and Busoni, Casals and Kreisler, for ninepence, seeing Little Tich and Grock for fourpence, reading H. M. Tomlinson in the local paper and Chesterton's Saturday essay in the *Daily News*, buying our shilling classics or Nelson's old sevenpenny series. I am not growling and grumbling again. For all I know to the contrary, lots of youngsters in their late teens are having as good a life now. Here I am not contrasting two periods. I am explaining why, in my considered judgment, these years, when I was neither in school nor college, turned out the most rewarding years I ever knew. It was, I repeat, because I was fortunate in my environment. It was not that I went to the right sort of school, but that I was living in the right sort of town. (Of course it might not have been right for you, but it was right for me.) In theory no doubt it was all wrong that a 'gifted youth' should spend his best years working long hours in a wool office. In practice it worked well. But it worked well, not because I happened to have massive determination and an iron will (I have never had either at any time), but because there was something in the atmosphere of that place at that period which encouraged me to develop and to grow. I do not think any school or college, by itself, could have done it. I would always have been wondering what was happening outside the walls. I would have been telling myself that this scholastic seclusion was not real life. I would not have taken anybody's word about what was going on in the outer world. But living as I did, I knew I was experiencing real life, exploring the outer world, taking what I wanted from my own town. Thus I was educating myself.

Let us take a look at what seem at first sight to be more formal processes of education. For example, at Oxford and

Cambridge. In what lies their unique value? I would reply without hesitation that it lies in their successful creation (not quite what it used to be, perhaps) of an atmosphere of disinterested scholarship, an environment in which thought itself is triumphant. A young man can live for at least nine terms in a place that does not care a damn about the price of cotton and tin and the export trade. He can sit up all night arguing about God and Art. He can lock himself in, as I did once, with a tin of tobacco, a case of beer, and the whole of the Elizabethan Drama. In such places knowledge is in the very air. Not the formal courses of instruction but the atmosphere and the surroundings enrich the student. I have long thought it a shame that our students of music and acting have to live in London, lost among millions who care little or nothing for these arts. They would do much better if, as sometimes happens abroad, they received instruction in some place where the very landladies and bus drivers had a passion for music or the theatre, where the street outside was the ally of the school.

Now we have to spend so much on the school that we cannot afford to civilise the street. We are hoping that sooner or later the school will be strong enough to overcome the street, that a generation of teenagers will finally leave school to tear down the street and rebuild the town. If you argue with enthusiastic educationalists, they will admit under pressure that so far the street seems to have won, but they will declare their faith in the imminent victory of the school. I wish I could share this faith. But the odds seem to me too heavily in favour of the street, the town, the local environment. If their influence is not good,

51

then the good influence of the school will not last long. To nine youngsters out of ten, the values of their home, their street, their town, seem far more important than anything learnt at school. There, outside, is real life, the world of the adults, towards which they are headed, away from the kid stuff of the classrooms. So it is largely a waste of time and money trying to persuade children that Shakespeare is our pride and joy if the town they live in cannot even boast one theatre, and prefers the films of Abbott and Costello to all that Shakespeare ever wrote. And if more and more youngsters leaving school want to read the *Daily Scream*, which steadily gets worse and worse, then what return is our national investment in education bringing? No doubt we need more teachers and should offer them better prospects. But what guarantee have we that they can successfully challenge the proprietors of the *Daily Scream*, the TV, radio and film experts, the advertising gang, the haters of the arts, the slow murderers of eager, hopeful living? Who, so far, is winning all along the line?

But no, I must not growl and grumble. I will simply state the case, as I see it. I owe most to a time when I was not being formally educated but when I enjoyed an environment favourable to a youth of my sort. I realise that youth still has its opportunities, perhaps more of them in some directions than I had, but it does seem to me that by and large the environment is far less favourable than it was, chiefly owing to the recent development of mass communications and of what might be called a mass pseudo-culture. (Where comparison can be made, for example, with the popular Press, the decline is obvious.) Meanwhile, we spend more and more and more on Education, hoping rather desperately that somehow and sometime the values of the school will triumph over those of the streets outside the school. And this costs us so much that we cannot afford to change and improve the towns that receive our boys and girls after they have left school. The environment they know in their later teens, probably their most formative years, is a dreary mess of cheap commercial values, in which any fire kindled in the classroom is likely to be soon damped down and smothered. Perhaps the educationalists are right, and we have only to turn a corner. Perhaps I am an odd fish and cannot argue from my own experience. But I cannot help feeling thankful that I grew up before we had achieved such progress.

THE NEWEST NOVELS

Whenever a novel by a young writer is given much praise, I buy it and read it. Thus I know the sort of fiction that is being written by the young and presumably is admired by them. If I do not mention names, that is not because I am bluffing, but because I am not one of the fiction critics of this paper and anyhow do not wish to get bogged down in literary criticism. But the names are in my mind, the books themselves either in this or the next room. And let me add here that I have never met any of the writers. I wish I had, though for the purpose of writing this piece I am better off without their acquaintance: I can concentrate on their work.

These novels have much in common. The New English Novel is now emerging. I am certain that the writers do not belong to a Group, with common aims, a manifesto, mutual criticism, as they almost surely would do if they were foreign novelists of the same age. And it is significant that they should be producing quite independently more or less the same sort of novel. It proves that the *Zeitgeist* is at work. Gifted and ambitious young fellow-citizens of ours are apparently looking at life and presenting their vision of it in the same fashion. What they see, feel, and think seems to me very important. We are always being told what politicians, economists, trade union leaders, industrialists, sociologists, and psychologists are thinking, and are perhaps a little weary of their questions, their protests, their conclusions. Let us try, if only for a change, some young people of literary talent. Why wait until they are eighty?

Without venturing into literary criticism, I will first admit that these novels have in my eyes two major weaknesses. The world they present does not seem to me quite real. I am never quite convinced that what they tell me is happening really is happening. It is rather like being in a dream and reminding oneself it *is* a dream. These pubs, these schools and colleges, these offices, these film studios, do not seem quite solidly set in the world I know. They are rather like stage scenery out of drawing and queerly coloured. But of course this proves nothing, except that I am in my sixtieth year and these writers are in their twenties and early thirties, that I am wedded to one convention and they are busy creating another. My second objection is that as a rule their central characters are too deliberately unheroic, and often seem such bumbling nitwits that it is hard to sympathise with them in their misfortunes. I do not ask for Double Firsts and Triple Blues who look like Gregory Peck, but some of these melancholy caddish clowns and oafs do seem to need a nurse or a probation officer rather than a chronicler and a reader. However, this again may be a change in convention: I think we may assume that these clever young people know what they are doing.

And what are they doing? They are saying in effect: "You go on making your arrangements or arguing about them. But count us out. We're not with you." I do not mean that there is a kind of militant anarchy in this fiction;

I wish there were. But this is something different, not to be easily included in the categories of my generation. These novels do not openly denounce and protest against the elaborate organisation and machinery of our society. They simply ignore them. It is almost as if a South Seas Islander were trying to live amongst us. The chief characters are like poachers on the vast game preserve of responsible citizenship. They are artful dodgers rather than open rebels, the type we older novelists have often presented. The wearisome obligations, about which we argue, seem to them like so many holes or blocks in the road, so much bad weather. Any public life of which we may catch a glimpse in these novels seems both remote and idiotic. This is essentially the fiction not only of private life but of a deeply introverted private life, to be hugged to oneself between back bedroom and bar parlour.

The only ambition of its central characters is to get by until a week on Tuesday. In a world of planners, they plan nothing. They would no more try for any sort of career than try for the Centre Court at Wimbledon. They stroll in and out of jobs, so many highbrow casual labourers. They do not seem to care what they do so long as it offers no future and they have not to take it seriously. They are gipsies in old pullovers and dirty raincoats. They care nothing about money. If they have some, they spend it on seedy binges or some odd extravagance; and if they have none, they go without, borrow from unlikely acquaintances, or take the first odd job that is going. They never seem to own anything except a battered little suitcase and a few gramophone records. They can hardly be said to live anywhere, though sometimes they occupy other people's flats and drink their liquor. They do not commit crimes but they appear to live at the same distance from ordinary citizenship as the habitual criminal does. They are equally far removed from the worlds of the *Daily Telegraph, Daily Express, Daily Herald,* or *Daily Worker.* They have some loves, a few odd friends, but no social group to which they belong. They are perhaps the most isolated and loneliest characters in all fiction. Their London is filled with packed buses and steaming tap-rooms and yet is a desert island on which they have been mysteriously wrecked.

It is impossible to imagine any of the major characters in these novels buying a house, bringing up children, paying taxes, organising a business, serving on a committee, standing for Parliament. They are simply not with us. They no more live in our political and economic world than children of six do. They are capable, of course, of arguing about our problems, and occasionally do after the fifth pint or whisky, but they do not share these problems, they exist quite outside them. It is as if already they were on the other side of the monstrous bombs threatening us. Nearly thirty years ago an odd novel by Romer Wilson attracted much attention: it was called *The Death of Society.* Now this latest fiction makes us feel that it is already happening. I suspect that most of these young writers have been much influenced by the French Existentialists, who chiefly arrived at their philosophy—or at least attitude of mind—during the Nazi Occupation, which in fact much helped to shape and colour it. And we might say that behind these novels there is a sort of Occupation Philosophy. But who in this case are the menacing forces against which there must be a secret Resistance Movement? The answer, I am afraid, is that we are—you and I, reader. Yes, they are against us.

They are not against us—and of course by 'us' I really mean the society we have created—in open rebellion, deciding to be Anarchists instead of Tories, Liberals, or Socialists. This in many ways would be less serious than what is actually happening, for they would still be playing our game, if for another side. But they are in fact refusing to play our game at all. They are quietly contracting out of our society altogether, not of course as persons but in their capacity as imaginative writers. They have deliberately made the world of their fiction the world that escapes the newspaper columns, the debates, the *Any Questions*. How do we go on—they are asking in effect—outside it all? What is it like not to be a responsible citizen, a thoughtful member of the electorate, a pillar of society? I do not say there is not a literary device here, a desire to avoid what is stale and wearisome, a flight to fresh fields. And there will be those, many of them with much influence, who will tell us that there is nothing here but literary devices, merely the tricks and shifts of entertainers who share with sodium amytal the task of helping serious responsible persons to sleep. I say this because not since the Wars of the Roses has literature been held in such low esteem. Any television mountebank is now more important than any poet, novelist, dramatist. But if our society is diminishing and pooh-poohing the writer, here, I repeat, are some new writers who are rejecting our society. And this is something more than an entertainer's trick, to give the show a new twist. It comes white-hot from the imagination. It is indeed what is most personal, most deeply sincere, in this fiction. At its very centre is the cry *Count us out!*

Now, as I began by declaring, these are the younger novelists who have been given most praise, who are attracting most attention. Which means, among other things, that theirs is a point of view that many other people, particularly round about their own age, find acceptable. Clearly they are not merely expressing their own thoughts and feelings. The eager response is here too. Compared with the vast ballyhoo of mass communications, all this may seem on a very small scale indeed, a tiny flurry in the review columns and the bookshops. But it is folly to imagine that the influence of the articulate, the literate, those who try to think and feel for themselves, can be estimated by counting their heads. Who are writing, praising, reading, these novels? The very people who in one form or another can influence a great many others. Take note, therefore, of what may be found in these new novels. This is what is being freshly and urgently thought and felt. This is how the imaginative young are looking at us and our society. Call their work merely so many straws in the air, if you like; but notice which way the wind is blowing.

THE REAL CLEAN-UP

Being greedy and self-indulgent, I often eat too much, and I smoke too much strong tobacco, with the result that I sleep badly. This means that I do a great deal of reading in bed. Literature and books that have ideas in them are no use to me as bed books because they excite me and make me more wakeful than ever. So I read a great many detective stories and thrillers of the better sort, most of which I borrow from our local bookshop library. Many of these, by writers unknown to me, I glance at and then throw aside, because they cannot be read even in the small hours. But this means that I take a dip into all manner of stuff, and do at least learn what is being written, published, and read.

It has been said that those of us who read fiction of this kind are secretly attracted to it by the violence it depicts. This, in my own case, I most stoutly deny. What attracts me to it, simply as bed reading, is that it offers me narrative on a certain artificial level, not unlike the *Arabian Nights*. I like narrative—and am no bad hand at it myself—and if it is free from challenging ideas and the oppressive but fascinating thickness of something like real life, then I skim along easily, with part of my mind sufficiently engrossed while the remainder of it prepares itself for sleep. A certain amount of violence is almost inevitable in stories that deal with crime and its detection, though I have long held that there is too much murder in such fiction, too many corpses and not sufficient ingenuity in offering us riddles not stained with blood. (For example, we are told that every year hundreds of people simply disappear. What stories could be told about them!) And, it must be remembered, some of our best novelists both here and in America are fascinated by violence: this is, after all, an age of violence. But as a reader—and certainly as a reader-in-bed—I am not attracted by it; and indeed most of the stories I throw aside sicken me because they describe, with a gusto missing from the rest of their narratives, scenes that descend to the depths of atrocity. Moreover, they ask not only for our interest but for our admiration. It is not just the villains who smash noses, gouge eyes, and beat people to a jelly; the heroes do it too, and indeed are handier at it than the villains. There is a familiar type of husky private detective who is better at getting results than the police are, just because he behaves like a member of the Gestapo or the S.S. And now, I am sorry to say, there seem to be even more of these tough guys in English than in American fiction.

This is not a good dream life to offer adolescent lads. Much of this fiction is of course aimed at them. The hero is what they would like to be. Outwardly he is everything they are not: tall, broad-shouldered, very strong, very brave, attractive to the girls; he is 'a snappy dresser', negligently drives a very fast car, drinks all manner of exotic stuff (he hardly ever eats), and strolls in and out of strange night-clubs, throwing pound notes about, not giving a damn for anybody except the enchanting blonde in the corner. And if you are seventeen, five foot four and rather puny, a victim of acne, with only two shabby suits, a job in a cheese warehouse, no entranced girls, two and eight-pence to last you until Friday, and several jeering brothers and sisters, then you want to live gloriously, if vicariously, with such a hero. Nothing new here: boys and youths have been identifying themselves with the Hero for thousands of years; this cannot be stopped. But we might see to it that the Hero is not so often kicking people in the stomach and then smashing their faces into red pulp. We do not want to find ourselves surrounded on a dark night by youths whose imaginations have been nourished on such scenes. It will be as well if the citizens of tomorrow do not take it for granted that people they dislike should be beaten, pounded, minced. The red-pulp view of life should be discouraged.

If some of our cleaners-up would stop thinking about sex and take a look at this violent, cruel stuff, they might yet do us a service. This is not likely to happen. It is the pleasures of sex and not the pains of cruelty that start the puritan crusading. The people who mark the spicy bits in their library books are probably not on the increase, but lately their complaints have been taken seriously by officials who used to have the sense to ignore them. Obviously, there is somewhere a great Cleaner-Up, who prefers not to see what a lot of nonsense is being written about obscenity and pornography in recent fiction. (One man in *The Times* claimed Mrs. Bloom's interior mono-logue, at the end of *Ulysses*, as a spicy-bit-de-luxe. Any-body who finds an aphrodisiac there is in no need of one.) You would imagine from all these complaints that sex can only be discovered in print, whereas there is so much sex in most people's heads that a writer would have to work very hard to put in any more. A youth of our time has not to read a book to find sexual stimulation: the lecherous eye is catered for by an army of experts; the whole landscape bulges with secondary female characteristics. Our films are most thoroughly examined and censored, with all those ten-foot bosoms being measured to an inch, but many of them contrive to be impersonally sexy to the point of nausea, turning whole cities into whore-houses. Our smaller music-halls, once the nurseries of genuine talent, are now chiefly given over to touring revues that exploit sex in the crudest and dreariest fashion, Aphrodite in dirty wool underwear. No doubt some writers of fiction, uncertain of their power to entertain and hard-pressed in a grimly competitive trade, try to compete with these other lascivious enterprises; but if I were in search of stimulus, I do not think I would sample the efforts of these colleagues.

I am doubtful myself of the artistic value of detailed descriptions of sexual acts, for reasons I have no space for here. I do not like much pornography, and never made a close friend of anybody who offered me the run of an expensive library of it (probably inherited from a Victorian; they were notable collectors); there is always something wrong with people who have too much sex in their heads. But this talk of 'sheer filth' and the terrible corruption of the young seems to me very silly, at least when applied to passages dealing with the straightforward commerce of the sexes. To such filth we owe our earthly being. And even the rubbishy sexual stuff in cheap fiction is not likely to harm most youngsters, soon to be confronted by the blazing urgency of their own sexual lives, in a society

63

already heavily committed to almost every trick of exploiting sex. The raging curiosity of the young is no recent product. In my time we searched the Bible and Shakespeare for passages to giggle over in secret. As for adults, if they prefer a sexual dream life, dubiously heightened by trashy novels, to the strenuous give-and-take of reality, then there is something so wrong with them that prosecuting a few writers and publishers will not help very much.

Nine youngsters out of ten will sooner or later discover sex for themselves, even if their favourite hero is not always being voluptuously entangled. But this cruel violence is something else. It is by no means an essential part of us. No doubt there is in us the germ of it, a spark of savagery, especially in youth. One of the aims of civilisation is to smother that spark, to provide an environment in which that germ cannot flourish and multiply. But here in this popular fiction the whole civilised trend is being carefully reversed. It is more than a question of manners. There is in much of our early fiction—in Fielding and Smollett, for example—a lot of rough-and-tumble, knockabout brutality, as much a reflection of its time as Hogarth's pictures were. But this new violence, with its sadistic overtones, is quite different. It is not simply coarse, brutal from a want of refinement and nerves, but genuinely corrupt, fundamentally unhealthy and evil. It does not suggest the fairground, the cattle market, the boxing booth, the horseplay of exuberant young males. It smells of concentration camps and the basements of secret police. There are screaming nerves in it. Its father is not an animal maleness but some sort of diseased manhood, perverted and rotten. And the writers who offer us this stuff—who must not be confused with those who are dealing fairly and frankly with the more violent aspects of contemporary life —give the game away by their gloating eagerness, the sudden heightening of their descriptive powers. And, let me repeat, in the stories of which I complain these sadistic antics are displayed for our admiration; it is the Hero, with whom the younger reader identifies himself, who is the master of them. Any lad who tries to forget his various frustrations by continually reading such stuff is in danger of real corruption. The results may be discovered in some of our Sunday papers.

What can we do about it? Well, in my view, it is not necessary to use the heavy machinery of the police and the law courts. The book trade can clean itself up. Writers, publishers' readers, publishers, reviewers, booksellers, can do most of the job between them. They have only to be honestly aware of this evil trend to begin putting a stop to it. Most people in our trade are decent enough not to want to make money out of corruption. If the writer still writes it, the publishers' readers should call his attention to it, the publishers should refuse to publish it, the reviewers should condemn it, the booksellers boycott it. We may be hard-pressed, as I believe we are, but not so far gone that we cannot do a little cleaning up ourselves. It is not hard to make a start. Not long ago I found one of the largest bookshops in the West End having a special counter display of a writer of this sadistic muck. I took the manager over to it and told him he ought to be ashamed of himself. The special display vanished. That was not much, but at least it was a beginning.

GREY EMINENCES

C. P. Snow's novel about the atomic scientists, *The New Men*, had been hiding itself beneath a lot of newer books, so I have only just finished reading it. A curious novel, it seems to me; very intelligent throughout and sharply perceptive here and there; but chilly and spectral, as if the bombs these fellows were about to make had all gone off, London and the Home Counties were a grave-yard, and we were all flitting from one committee of ghosts to another. I do not know if Mr. Snow, who usually knows what he is about, intended to create such a cold grey atmosphere, and it is not my purpose here to decide that or to criticise him. But as I read him I began to be haunted by a query that has not left me yet and that might be worth some brief examination. To some readers, no doubt, this query and all I say about it will seem fanciful, but before such readers pass on to chew and digest stronger meat, I would ask them to remember the strange character of our age, how it refuses to be explained by any amount of nineteenth-century political theory. Indeed, most of our chief mistakes have probably been the result of this in-adequate and outworn theorising. We need Dr. Jung, not the ghost of Lord Morley.

While still feeling repelled by the chill greyness Mr. Snow discovered for me, I began to wonder about these new men of his, now exercising such power over us, incidentally without having received any mandate from most of us. (Those who condemn mankind for being so wickedly aggressive might remember that no representative bodies of citizens anywhere have ever demanded that atomic and hydrogen bombs should be manufactured and used. They are here not because we are like wolves but because we are more like hypnotised sheep. Our grandfathers would have destroyed any Government that behaved so monstrously.) I asked myself if these were the sort of men who should have so much power. Of course scientists outside their laboratories are varied types, ranging from thin-lipped high priests to roaring double-whisky boys. But it may be that a certain type, with a certain background, may tend to prevail among them, as Mr. Snow, perhaps unconsciously, suggests; and about this type I have some doubts. I do not know that I want our lives to be shaped by him. He does not seem to me the man for the job.

He is now, we will say (without having any actual physicist in mind), Sir Nuclear Fission, and we are shown press photographs of him about to climb into an aeroplane that will take him to some distant explosion, and in these photographs he can even wear a grin, though what he has to grin about is a mystery to me, for his are antics about which it would be better to keep a straight face. Now let us go back, hazarding guesses not entirely without foundation but still with no actual man in mind. Nuclear is born of shop-and-chapel people in one of the dingier suburbs of South London, Birmingham, Manchester, one of those late-Victorian wildernesses of trams and soot, cheap sweets and racing papers. In some grim secondary school, looking like a boot factory, he gobbles up all the general and scientific education offered him, a determined and not very companionable lad, perhaps cut off from boys' games and nonsense by a studious disposition, short sight, and a desire not to be a grumbling failure like his father. In intellect he is already beyond his age, but in the richness, variety, colour and tang of boyhood experience he is well behind it. He has some suspicion of this, but is not worried about it, for life will really begin somewhere else, far from these familiar shabby streets.

He wins a scholarship that at least enables him to exist, if not to live, at a university, where again, free from so many temptations to make a gorgeous ass of himself, he soon learns all that his professors can teach him and is regarded as a brilliant man, which indeed from one point of view he undoubtedly is. He has few friends, and those few are of his own sort, to whom Science offers a chance to forget the profound dissatisfactions of daily life. In one world he is a rather seedy, shy youth, hurrying from digs to lab, whereas in the other, with its glittering palaces of intellectual certainties, its beckoning vistas of unconquered provinces, he is a proud young prince. It is now about 1930, a lean time, which awards him a badly paid assistant-professorship in another university, a gloomy red-brick job. The odds are that he lives in uncomfortable digs, a long tram-ride from anything that looks like civilisation, nourishes himself chiefly on stewed tea, weak coffee, dry sandwiches, shepherd's pie, prunes and custard, and smokes a mixture of tobacco dust and saltpetre. While he is beginning to explore the atom—and we must not deny him the magic of that experience—the primroses are thick in the lanes, the bluebells glimmer and fade in the woods, nightingales sing to the moon, lovely girls loll among king-cups, the fish are rising in distant lakes, ancient bar parlours are dark and cool in hot noons, lucky men are staring at strange beautiful eyes above decanters of Chambertin, old rogues in country houses have filled themselves with sirloin and cheese soufflé and are now lighting *Partagas* on the terrace; but all this is happening a long way from Dr. N. Fission, who, outside his lab and the common room, is living the life of an ant in a dustbin.

However, disregarding the claims of the frustrated senses, he makes progress in his work, perhaps driven all the harder by a certain mysterious bitterness. Finally, when a small team of first-class research men is needed for top-secret-highest-priority-hush-hush-between-these-four-walls-old-man work, Fission is demanded. He is now, at last, coming into his kingdom. He leaves his dingy suburban digs and lecture-rooms and labs and baked beans on toast and crowded buses and wet raincoats and urban squalor, and is taken into the country. But only to disappear into a compound, not unlike a small prisoner-of-war camp. Indeed, he might be said to be a prisoner-of-war, but of course he is better paid and more comfortable than he was, can afford such luxuries and entertainment, no doubt, as he needs. Perhaps by this time he is married. Now—young feminine readers please note (what a shame if I have none!)—much depends on Mrs. Fission. Let us hope she was not one of his third-year students and his female counterpart but, by a lucky chance, a sumptuous lass, with a rich sensuous nature, much subtlety and witch-craft, a passion for the fruits of the earth and making love.

F

If she is, she can teach him to appreciate and feel a tenderness for actual warm, breathing life, the feathers and fur and hair of living creatures. She can restore to him that natural piety of feeling he lost so long ago.

If his wife cannot do it, or if there is no woman with him, then there is a danger that Sir Nuclear, as he is now, will bring to the tasks he has been given, to the power he now possesses, a temperament that has been warped by frustration, a mind that is brilliant but unbalanced and that moves almost entirely among abstractions which seem to have more essential reality, to be closer to the heart of things, than the daylight outside, the trees and the grass, the living forms. Such a man, all by way of doing his duty, might get up to anything. Indeed, as we know only too well, though most of us probably do not know the half of it yet, he has.

This is not an attack on Science, nor even on most scientists. I am not saying that Sir Nuclear, the bad case, is a worse human being than the rest of us are. In many respects he is much better. His industry, his patience, his skill, his single-minded and selfless devotion to his work, might easily make us feel small and frivolous. Nevertheless, through no fault of his own, he may prove to be one of the most dangerous members of our society just because he has now so much power and has arrived at it in such an arid, chill, and frustrating fashion. The earth and its living creatures may not be real to him. He has been compelled to starve both his senses and his imagination. He can easily undervalue life because he has never really lived it. He may indeed secretly dislike what he knows of it, as we might too in his place. After all, what has the world, as

revealed to the senses, offered him? So, though the sensual-
ist may ruin himself, this non-sensualist may ruin a continent. He could blunder into it because, strictly speaking,
he does not know what he is doing. In the largest possible
meaning of the term, he is out of touch. So, in the most
helpful fashion, as a good citizen, he will suggest devices
that make our blood run cold. But then his blood is
already cold.

Every Sunday, from ten thousand pulpits, people are
still being warned against the snares of the senses as if they
were not weary tractor-drivers and anæmic housewives
but Caliphs of Baghdad who had only to clap their hands
to start illimitable orgies. Too many of our theologians
and moralists, forgetting this is another age, another
climate, have imaginations still haunted by glaring Eastern
suns, troupes of painted dancing girls, rose petals snowing
on the wine jars, Dionysian debaucheries, temples of
Ashtoreth, altars and fires of Baal and Moloch. There is
more danger now from senses that are starved rather than
over-indulged, from a lack of a richly sensuous way of
living, from thin, cold temperaments bred in our warrens
of cement, with no natural feeling for all that is warm and
alive, with no imagination, no gratitude, no tenderness for
life. We must beware the revenge of the starved senses,
the embittered animal in its prison. Turn from the ten
thousand pulpits to the ten million copies of the popular
Sunday Press: its gross sensationalism, to which so much
dignity and decency are sacrificed, responds to a need that
is rooted in this feeling of frustration, felt by people in the
urban mass who, acting as a crowd, a public, make
demands they would still be ashamed to make in their

own private lives. If they have to count the tears of the murderer's mother, or look at the legs of the victim's widow, or have some poor wretch hounded into a hospital or asylum, we must remember these people have been cut off from so much, lack so many primary satisfactions. They have been herded away from the rich, warm stream of life. You can have a refrigerator, a washing machine, an electric toaster, a TV set, and still be in prison.

At the same time we may be producing, out of these faceless ranks, more and more men of exceptional ability, like our scientist, who fill positions of importance, obtain influence and power, as politicians, bureaucrats, planners, business executives, strategists, propagandists, and who seize this power all the more avidly because there is so little else in their lives. Many of them will be hopelessly one-sided, over-developed simply as brain workers and miserably under-developed as experiencing sympathetic natures. They have knowledge without a correspondence level of being. They exist almost entirely in a barren middle ground, being neither good animals nor lovers, poets, sages, seers. They understand graphs, statistics, plans, public opinion reports, but not the life of man. Already some of them are compressing the structure of our lives and draining the colour out of them. Give others a little more time and rope, and those of us who are left will all live underground, below plains of concrete where not one bird sings, doing our best to get along with dwarfs, giants and brand-new experimental types (*Worker, Class D.*5) with pointed heads and eight arms.

SACRED
WHITE ELEPHANTS

Not long ago, a song had to be cut out of the revue, *Light Fantastic*, by order of the Lord Chamberlain. I happened to read the lyric—or most of it—and it described the plight of Mr. Eden:

> Thirty-odd years of frustrated desire
> Waiting for senior men to retire. . . .

It seemed very mild satire, not to be compared with the Britten number at the Court Theatre or with what has been done to many of us in our time. There is, however, one important difference. The victim of this lyric is a politician, and the time has arrived when we must not poke fun at politicians. They can be rough with us but we must not be rough with them. They are the sacred white elephants of our era.

If you do not like the world we are living in now, please remember that it is largely the creation of politicians, with some help from the bureaucrats they command. They spend much of their time trying to make us forget this. They have a trick of suggesting that by prodigies of states-manlike thought and action they will shortly rescue us from the pits into which we have so carelessly fallen. It is never suggested that they dug the pits and perhaps pushed

73

us in. If the news is bad, somehow it is our fault, but they will do their best for us. If the news is better, we owe it to them.

Chancellors of the Exchequer, smirking at you on Budget Day, are afraid they "cannot give you much this time". It does not seem to occur to them that they have never given us anything, that they are talking about our money and not theirs. There was a time when the House of Commons was there to give grudging consent to taxes being raised, duties levied, and public money being spent. Now it is filled with men who decide what they would like to spend and then compel us to find the money. In a sensible age we should decide what the Government was worth, allot it so much money and tell it to make that do. But we cannot do that because we are now kept permanently terrified. It is our money or our life.

I do not blame our politicians for asking more pay for themselves, not when prices are always rising. But not one of them, including a Prime Minister who calls himself an author, has had the decency to raise the question of Civil List pensions, those awards for distinguished service to the community. They are now on a scale that will barely keep an elderly man or woman alive. An artist in his prosperous days might pay enough in taxes to maintain a dozen politicians, but if later, weary and out of favour, he should face destitution, these same fellows will toss him two hundred a year and ask for his gratitude. Monarchs whose meanness was legendary did better than this. But then the political view is that we do not need artists. If we are in search of style, wit, and humour, we can read *Hansard*. The clashes between Messrs. Butler, Macmillan, Attlee,

74

and Bevan offer us all the drama we need. Sir Winston can supply both water-colours and oils.

We should remember that Communist leaders are politicians too. They are politicians with the lid off. They have arrived where most of our politicians would like to be. They are wiser, stronger, handsomer, than any other human beings who ever lived; they know more about all the arts than the artists; they can dictate philosophy to the philosophers before breakfast; their portraits, as the world's noblest benefactors, must be hung everywhere so that the happy people can stare at them through a mist of tearful gratitude. In short, with some help from the secret police, they have succeeded in putting over the greatest con-fidence-trick swindle of all time.

Our politicians may have no such conceit of themselves, but already they must not be laughed at, and are as deeply concerned about their rights and privileges as they are in-different to so many of ours. I am under the impression that even here the gap between the politician and the ordinary fool of a citizen is widening all the time. One makes the rules, and the other obeys them. If everybody had to obey them, there might be fewer rules. I should like to see some of the people who insist upon our having passports, visas, currency control, fall in at the end of the queue instead of walking past it, smiling and free. Notice how, having made most forms of travel as difficult as possible for ordinary citizens, the politicians seem to do more and more travelling, chiefly at somebody else's expense.

Notice, too, how the politician is now the representative man, the chief exhibit. It is possible to imagine that foreigners, interested in Britain and the British, might like to meet such Britons as Vaughan Williams, Augustus John, Bliss, Walton, Henry Moore, Bertrand Russell, Walter de la Mare, Joyce Cary, Graham Greene, Benjamin Britten, and so on and so forth. But whether they are visiting us here or entertaining us at home, these interested foreigners get politicians, almost every time. If not senior and important politicians, then back-benchers will have to do, however dim and dreary. The member for North Coketown can represent the island race. For after all, the argument must run, even the dimmest and dreariest politician is more important, more truly representative, than anybody else. If the encounter is not political, then what is it? Nothing worth mentioning.

Have you ever, my dear voter, my dear taxpayer, my dear innocent, sat at a dining-table with politicians of different parties, men ready to denounce one another at the drop of a chairman's hand? It is an illuminating experience. The real gulf is not between them but between you and them. It is you they do not understand nor want to understand. They are close to and delighted with one another. They live in the same cosy world. They face the same professional problems, suffer from the same occupational diseases, talk more or less the same claptrap. They admire one another. No doubt the economics of the other side are unsound, the foreign policy dubious—but what brilliance, what wit, what noble eloquence, what magnificent service to the country!

In a world shaped and coloured more and more by politicians, the nations meet politically—and hardly any other way—to settle their differences. It is hard going. It could not be anything else. Men who have spent most of their adult lives plotting and jockeying for place and power meet other men who have been doing the same thing, all of them riddled with the same occupational disease. After looking specially stern and noble—or confident and smiling —for the photographers, these harassed men climb into aircraft, to be dropped down to argue with other politicians in expensive villas, chiefly paid for by men who can no longer afford a second pair of shoes. Day and night they toil to bring us peace, a chance of lasting prosperity. I do not doubt their sincerity. But I cannot help wondering sometimes if the wrong people are not trying to do the job, if it might not be better if some other people were given *carte blanche* to have a good try. These other people might not be accustomed to thinking in terms of power and conflict, might not be condemned to pursue policies that must result in an inevitable clash, might just want to have done with the whole weary business so that *they could get on with something else.*

I know the politician says he wants to get on with something else. But often he has been dipped too deep. He no longer knows what that something else could be. He cannot imagine any other mode of life. And men who have long pursued and then enjoyed power cannot bear to lose it. Here even the emperors—a Tiberius, a Diocletian, a Charles the Fifth—made a better showing than the politicians, who cling to power though their hands are trembling claws. If they let go, they feel their real life is over. They may tell us—and themselves—that they look forward to obscurity and a rose garden; but the world that lights them up in the centre of the stage, that hangs upon

77

their pronouncements, that rushes them here and there to save the situation at the last moment, that offers them platforms, conferences, midnight intrigues, an excited Press, unnumbered followers, power and glory, is the true mirror of their mind and heart.

This is one reason why we now live in a world of crises, of scare headlines, of sudden alarms and deepening uncertainties. The ordinary sensible citizen, who does not want power and glory but a quiet life, has less and less control over this world. It is one he never made. It does not reflect him at all. But whatever he may say, the careerist politician is completely and happily at home in it. In his heart of hearts he does not really want to change it. Consciously he may desire peace, quiet, an easy prosperity from here to Harbin; but there must be times when his unconscious clamours for more and more crises, either abroad or at home, a world in tumult, a civilisation he can be busy saving while indulging himself royally. It has often been observed that the Communist leaders, while they may not actually want war, have no genuine desire for the peaceful settlements, the safe and friendly world, they are always talking about. Quite so. But then the Communist leaders are professional politicians with the lid off.

Take all these politicians out of this crisis atmosphere, or out of the game and gambles and improvised dramas of party politics, and see how naked they look. Where are the insights, the long views, the wisdom? Remove from their speeches the immediate irritants, the play on prejudices and fears, the doses of soothing syrup, and what have you left? Read the pitiful books they write, chapter after chapter of platitude, catch-phrases, and claptrap, so that you wonder how they can imagine such stuff can match the dignity they claim. Where among them, in any major country, do you find even the ghost of an idea for saving our civilisation? During these last few years I have read and heard much—thank God—that made me feel there is still a hope for us, but never once was it a politician who was writing or talking.

I shall be told I am asking too much from men in the dusty arena of affairs. But I am taking them at their own valuation. On that level they condemn themselves. There was a time when politicians made no great claims; they attended as best they could to the nation's housekeeping and security; they made no pretence of being the representative men of their age; they did not tell other men how they ought to live, nor consider themselves entitled to all manner of special privileges, nor demand everybody's respectful attention all the time. But the Communists, in whose lives politics are the cancer, have set the pace for our world. If the Reds have leaders fifty feet tall, then we anti-Reds must have giant leaders too, ten feet this year, twenty feet next; and all the time for the rest of us the barbed wire rises and more and more gates are slammed in our faces.

ANOTHER
REVOLUTION

The other day, reading the Prologue to Collingwood's *Speculum Mentis*, I came to the following passage: "The actual output of pictures and statues, poems and string quartets does not fail of its market because of its own low quality; for the purchasers do not buy the best, because they have not the skill to distinguish it; and anyone who doubts this can prove it to himself by merely walking round an exhibition of pictures and observing which of them are marked with red seals. . . ." This was written just over thirty years ago. Now I have walked round a good many exhibitions of pictures during the last ten years, often prepared to buy something I particularly liked, and it has been my experience that after the first few days, in an exhibition that is selling at all, it is undoubtedly the best pictures that bear the red seals and have already been bought. The purchasers have changed since Collingwood's time. They have probably less money but they have better taste and judgment. There has in fact been a revolution that, so far as I know, no social philosopher anticipated, and that even now deserves more attention than it has received. And it might save some of us a good deal of time and temper if we understood what has happened and is still happening.

I do not know what is happening to other nations, but

I am certain that among us English the visual appreciation of things has increased while the literary sense is
decaying. Years ago I noticed that my own children lived
more through the eye than I had done at their age, and
that at the same time they did not lose themselves in books
as I had done. It did not occur to me then that perhaps a
general shift of attention was taking place. Now I am sure
that what had happened in my family had also happened
in thousands of others. These post-war years have shown
us the results of this change. Whatever appeals first to the
eye attracts immediate attention. The important art exhibitions, as we have seen, draw big crowds at once. Even
the more modest shows, if they are fairly representative,
are always well filled. More and more art books are published and sold, in spite of their high cost. There are more
and more books in which the text is a mere excuse for the
photographs. It is the popular illustrated periodicals that
survive. People must have something to stare at, as the
advertisers know. It is the demands of the eye that must
be satisfied first. What was once chiefly the method of the
kindergarten, to catch the attention of very young children,
is now imitated far and wide, for every possible purpose.

Post-war entertainment proves the point over and over
again. Ballet uses music, but its chief appeal is to the eye,
and the popularity of ballet shows no sign of waning.
(Even here in the Isle of Wight, where we do not even
pretend to be in the movement, the only Arts Council im-
port that paid for itself, I understand, was rather sketchy
ballet.) The ice shows, which play to fantastic business,
pipe out some indifferent words and music, but they are of
course designed for the eye. In order to survive at all, the

Theatre, especially in its larger productions, has had to seduce the visual sense, whatever might happen to the mind behind it. The most successful directors are visual directors, often working as if they were producing ballet and not drama. It is this fashion that is working havoc with some Shakespeare productions, which will omit some of his most exquisite poetry so that there is more time for pageantry and eye-filling antics. The Bard has almost been turned into a clothes-line. His newest directors, who seem to have no feeling for words, are ready to cut any other line.

The Film may have lost some ground as all-round entertainment during these last few years, but as a modest art form, as a visual creation of director and cameraman, it attracts more and more of the young. This is proved by the success of the British Film Institute and the hundred-and-one local societies it encourages. From the ballet the young London highbrows go swarming to any West End cinema showing a film that has been praised by the more austere critics, those concerned with visual values. Very few of these youngsters are to be found at any unspectacular play, no matter how original and powerful it might be. They no longer want words and ideas, not even those of Messrs. Eliot and Fry. The visual sense must be fed and satisfied: they must have objective images, beautiful and significant if possible, but at a pinch almost any will do.

Finally—as the film boys say, the Big Pay-off—Television. Notice that it exists continually in a champagne atmosphere of ballyhoo and excitement that sound radio, even in its greatest days, never knew. Make two successful appearances in *Who's Your Father?* and the red carpets are rolled out from Lime Grove to the Caprice Restaurant. Here is the Giant Eye in fine frenzy rolling. One turn of a switch, and the images pour in. True, there may be words and music—and I will delightedly grant you that now this is anything but a 'land without music'—but ask any television producer what his first concern is. It is the visual sense that must be tickled and flattered first. And with this medium, delivered on any hearth-rug, we are as yet only making a rough-and-ready start: a choice of programmes, larger screens, colour and closer definition, all are yet to come and all have been promised. And because its own chief appeal is to the eye, then its programmes will tend to emphasise more and more what appeals to the eye in the world outside. The children are its slaves. So a huge generation not of readers or listeners but of viewers is now moving towards what we hope can be called maturity. Unless there should be a sharp reaction—always a possibility among us pendulum creatures—the final triumph of the visual sense is assured. In the end will be The Eye.

If you are looking at pictures, photographs, ballet, ice shows and other spectacles, films and television programmes, you cannot be curled up in a chair with a book. Moreover, the mind finds it hard to use its interior eye with a lot of noise about, and quiet corners are harder to find than they used to be. (Sooner or later, some of us will have to buy an instrument that can switch on silence instead of sound.) Indeed, many youngsters are now so accustomed to noise that a quiet room seems sinister and they have to bring a radio set or a gramophone into it, for sheer security's sake. In this atmosphere it is impossible for the art of literature to flourish. All the conditions and habits of mind are against it. The inner eye cannot be exercised. A feeling for words, a sense of their magical potency, can no longer be acquired. Some interest in ideas, on which the appreciation of literature also depends, is hardly felt at all. (It has been noted by educators, particularly in America, that too much visual instruction can make a youngster's mind unfit to grapple with abstract ideas.) So the necessary equipment of a genuine reader has not been assembled. The password that opens the old treasure cave has been forgotten.

Here some critics, in my view, do more harm than good. These are the critics who take a lofty and somewhat arrogant stand, and seem to regard themselves as the ferocious theologians and grand inquisitors of the art. They announce, with that air of cold finality which impresses undergraduates and repels their fathers and mothers, that only a few books by a few carefully chosen authors can be regarded as Literature, and that all else is rubbish on which no time should be wasted. (The critic's own works, presumably, are an exception.) Thus, Stendhal is Literature, Dumas is not; Henry James is Literature, W. W. Jacobs is not. And nothing is gained, but much lost, by this hoity-toity treatment. It is better to assume that all writing not merely informative, all poems, novels, essays, even criticism, are *literature of a sort*, ranging from the shockingly bad to the good and glorious. A lad who has enjoyed Dumas may come to enjoy Stendhal. Jacobs, a genuine artist in his own kind, may lead to James. Because, in my youth, a lot of girls received at Christmas and birthdays their limp-leather editions of FitzGerald's

Omar, many of them went on to buy and read newer poets, with the result that poetry found its way into the lists of all good publishers. So long as there are readers, trying this and that, there is hope for literature. It has been our misfortune that just when reading itself, as a pleasurable activity, was challenged, when the easier visual sense began to be immensely catered for, we should have developed a school of critics who spent more time warning people away from literature than encouraging them to enjoy it. They were the allies of the outer, not the inner, eye. If they are now appalled by the success of these visual things, partly at the expense of literature, it serves them right: they helped to steer people away from the bookshops.

Books come out, of course, and by the thousand, and publishers strangely multiply, to swell the chorus of *Ruin*! But it cannot be denied that we no longer behave as if we were primarily a literary nation. The space given to books and authors has dwindled. The mere attention, let alone the old excitement, is not what it was. (Dylan Thomas's tragic early death, more than his life and works, gave him sudden prominence.) To a writer the atmosphere of Paris seems quite strange now, because Paris is still a literary capital and London is not. Sartre, no towering genius, is capable of generating more excitement on both banks of the Seine than all of us could raise here, even if the whole Council of the Society of Authors marched along the Embankment in our underpants, making a last desperate appeal to the visual if not to the literary sense. The grim harrying of the educated middle-class, which has long been both the chief producer and consumer of literature, has done something for this revolution too. If our rulers were to be photographed holding a book instead of patting a racehorse, both the important political sections of our people, the magnates and the trade unionists, would feel that some contact with the great heart of the nation had been lost. But even what is left of that middle class, which has given us most of these bearded young men and untidy girls with horse-tail hair, has been seduced by the visual appeal, is growing up to expect its images to be created for it, is forgetting the ancient magic of words and any passion for ideas. Sometimes I think they are being encouraged to go this way—for it is not our old art that receives the subsidies—because they will be all the easier to handle. The busy eye is less rebellious than the lively mind. No barricades will be manned by *montage* enthusiasts, balleto-manes, and the patrons of *Desert Song on Ice*. (And if publishers think they can still discover a few lively minds, what about putting a few of them in the dock, to be bullied by lawyers, then fined or imprisoned? That ought to rattle these fellows.) Meanwhile, we writers must accept the fact of this revolution. Soon we may have to take in one another's washing. It will be a change from trying to cut one another's throats.

SOMETHING ELSE

Much of the dissatisfaction so many of us express now, in writing, in our talk, even in our behaviour (I try to avoid that one), seems to me to have nothing to do with what we write, talk, or fuss about. We feel the dissatisfaction, the ache of disappointment, the irritating sense of frustration, the anger at having somehow been mysteriously cheated, and we try to find sensible reasons, usually on a newspaper topic level. The Russians! The Americans! The French! Churchill! Bevan! Rising prices! Taxes! State of literature, the theatre, the arts, anything! Of course, we have plenty of excuses. Look at the strain of modern living! Look at the advertisers who remind us of the strain of modern living! Look at the people who write about the advertisers who remind us of the strain of modern living! We could go on and on and on. And yet, when all allowance has been made, there is Something Else.

It is this Something Else that is stoking the furnaces far below, making our faces so red and angry, lifting our voices an octave or so. The gigantic sales of booze nowadays—and I buy and consume my share—owe much to this Something Else. It is odd, by the way, how unrealistic most people are about our present drinking habits. Thus, when I produced a novel called *Festival at Farbridge*, several people, including the late Cyril Joad, who liked the book and wrote to tell me so, protested that I had made my characters drink far too much. Now it is true they drank a good deal, but I doubt if they drank as much as many people of the same type do in real life. We middle-class English are steadily pickling ourselves. If we do not cut such a drunken figure in the world's eye as some other nations do, that is because our heads are stronger. I know delicate fair ladies who, without disarranging a wisp of hair or misplacing a syllable, can put away an amount of hard liquor that would send an old-fashioned navvy under the table. There are men among us doing important jobs, and doing them well too, who have not been strictly sober for years. Every new enterprise now is launched on a flood of dry Martinis, pink gins, and double Scotches. It is the labouring and artisan classes, busy saving for a larger TV set, fortnights at holiday camps, coach trips to spectacular occasions, who now represent temperance and sobriety. The professional and managerial types lap up the booze like sailors on leave. This is not all mere habit—though it plays a part, of course—for much of it, I feel, and especially the final tippling, the Ones For The Road, comes from an attempt to drown the conviction that there is Something Else, something that ought to be there, lighting up the evening, but just isn't. It is, much of it, that kind of drinking, not out of high spirits, like the occasional wild sprees of youth, but born of a lowered vitality, of disappointment, of melancholy disillusion. Again, it is mostly found among the middle-aged, though the young take to it fairly soon.

At this point, I can assume there has been an interruption. This Something Else, I am told, is a living religion, without which our lives are incomplete. And I

agree. But only with some reservations that will be un-
welcome. A religion that arrived like some great burning
vision would make this talk of Something Else seem foolish
babble. And, of course, there are men and women who
have found all they want in existing creeds. But they are
not the men and women I am describing, and among the
latter are converts—often enthusiastic, according to their
statements—to old faiths. Nevertheless, they are as much
the victims of Something Else as the rest of us are. There
they are, faith or no faith, looking rather glazed as the
evening drags on, shrugging their shoulders, accepting
another round or deciding—and what a queer touch of
despair there is in the familiar phrase—"to call it a day".
No doubt they are wrong to behave like this; no doubt
their faith condemns such behaviour. But that is in fact
how they do behave, like the rest of us—and often a bit
worse. And now, sir or madam, unless you have some
great burning vision with you, unless you can in a thunder-
flash make us fall in love with life and one another together, pray allow me to continue about this teasing
Something Else.

You have your friends in. They are their usual delight-
ful selves. Nothing goes wrong. There is some argument,
but not too heated; opinions, impressions, stories, are exchanged; common friends, doubtful acquaintances, work,
politics, new books, plays, films, are discussed; you laugh
at their jokes, they laugh at yours; joint excursions are
planned; all is easy and companionable, rosy and warm
against the black night. Yet when they have gone, when
you are emptying the ash trays or washing the glasses, you
feel once again that the evening was smaller, dimmer,

more routine, than it ought to have been, that some mysterious but vital element was missing. For this you can blame neither yourself nor your friends, though there are ugly moments when you tell yourself that perhaps you have seen too much of the So-and-Sos, that his egoism and her determined prattle are becoming rather hard to take. As a rule, however, you know that it is nobody's fault. Nor can you imagine what it is you have missed. You never expected nor desired a drunken orgy; or an evening in the German Romantic style, with eternal friendship being sworn as the tears ran down your cheeks; or an occasion studded with jewels of wit in the best eighteenth-century French manner; or some symposium of beautifully cadenced speeches on Good and Evil, the Sublime, the Soul, and the Everlasting Ideas. What, then, did you want that the evening never brought you? Wistful and idiotic, you can only mutter: . . . *I dunno* . . . *I dunno* . . . *Something Else.* . . .

It is the same if you have an evening out. You have been working hard and well, perhaps there is something to celebrate, so you take your beloved to the theatre. Not, of course, to the usual stale rubbish, concocted with one eye on coach parties from Luton. No, no, this is the real thing: perhaps the great Dame Edith is in command, at once sublimely majestic and infinitely adroit; or the enchanting Peggy, like some embodiment of the Magic Flute; or the earthy yet elfin Sir Ralph, a Bottom for ever haunted by Titania; or the protean Alec with the same clear flame of intelligence illuminating each character: it is all as good as we can make it now. You come out into the old sardonic night bubbling and chattering in praise of the star, the

whole cast, the production, the director, the scene designer, even the author if you want to go to that length.
You will tell your friends they must see this piece, you will
try to see it again yourself, enjoy another good evening.
Yes, a good evening, no doubt of that. No, no, couldn't
have been better! Wonderful, really! And yet . . . and
yet. . . . So once again there falls across your mind, its
surface glossy with forced enthusiasm, the shadow of that
Something Else.

Films, opera, ballet, music-halls, parties, fancy occasions
—but why go on? I will, however, add this about myself
—that now the shadow falls for me even on a night of
music. I hate to confess it, but truth compels me to. I
have not spent as much time with music as I have with
literature and cannot pretend to the same knowledge of it.
But it has always seemed to me—perhaps because I have
not had to wrest a livelihood out of it—the most rewarding, inspiring, *cleansing*, of the arts. The last thing I ever
heard Arnold Bennett say was after one of Toscanini's first
concerts at the Queen's Hall, of blessed memory. He
didn't like me—alas—but now and again he let up. After
Toscanini's *Eroica* had shown us the stature of our souls, he
could forget in his essential decency the dogfight of professional authorship, and he cried in his queer staccato
high-pitched fashion: "Gives us—a lift—doesn't it?" And
many a lift indeed this noble art has given me, so that I
have come floating out of concerts feeling more like a
radiant spirit than a heavy little bag of blood and guts,
envy and malice. I am always grumbling and growling in
these columns, until some people must feel that nothing
that happens now, no manifestation of this age, could ever

please me; but here I will declare that our recording and reproduction of music, the work of our scientists and technicians, brings us a gift so precious that it almost redeems the noise and idiocy of the time. To sit late, as I did the other night over a greying log, and absorb Schubert's Quintet in C, that last and noblest work, exploring a depth of tenderness far beyond the reach of words, alone with it, free from the distraction, the stir and creak of an audience, with nobody to mark how moved I was—why, this is to receive a benediction from the laboratories, where a thousand experts have worried a million cigarettes so that at last spirit should seem to cry to spirit. And no darkening and chilling reminder of Something Else on this occasion, I grant you. But at concerts, full-blown with humanity and rattling hard with applause, once so flawless and golden even though doomsday came thundering through the brass and kettledrums, now the shadow falls. They are good still, but they are not Something Else.

And now for it. If I have no explanation to offer, then all is whimsy-whamsy. Courage, courage! There are two clues. The first I have already indicated. We lack, we Something Elsers, the unifying force of a strong religious faith. Where the central-heating furnace ought to be in the basement is a dark, cold, empty space. Our lives have no sacred common ground. Some essential links, even within ourselves as well as with others, are missing. We cannot see one another as subjects of the same invisible kingdom. We are not ourselves all of a piece. So much is admitted: when the vision blazes again, there will be no more talk of Something Else. Meanwhile, let us examine the second clue. I said that the shadow did not fall, there was no cold gap in the experience, when I was sitting late listening to Schubert. And why not? Because, I suggest, here for me things usually separated were newly combined. It was not nine o'clock in a concert hall but midnight at home. In place of the usual book were those five instruments, murmuring and weaving. The instance is a small one, nevertheless the clue is there. Dissatisfaction seeps through because the patterns, fixed for so long, are becoming worn. I do not merely mean that they have been fixed so long for me individually, though my own age is not without its influence and I would not expect a lad of eighteen to feel the same. But even he would not feel as secure and happy with them as he would have done fifty or a hundred years ago. Not boredom—for that I do not defend—but this faint but persistent unease, this feeling that experience falls short of expectation, will trouble him long before it would have visited his forefathers. We need to break the patterns, to combine good things in new ways. Perhaps our friends ought to come and act for us or paint us. Perhaps we ought to crowd round the stage and exchange speeches with Dame Edith or Sir Ralph. Perhaps Bertrand Russell ought to help the Sadler's Wells Ballet, and Arnold Toynbee appear with the Philharmonia Orchestra. Perhaps we ought to rehearse our dinner parties and extemporise our stage performances. Perhaps novels ought to be a mixture of printed pages and recordings. Perhaps film and TV scripts ought to be written by metaphysicians, mad clergymen, and women who have kept low drinking dens. Perhaps Mills's Circus and the Royal Society could work something out together. I don't know. But I know there could be, must be, Something Else.

93

END OF A PARTY

It happened the night before we flew back from New York, at the long tail-end of a party, high above the East River. They were nice people, clever people, good liberals all, but suddenly my interest in the talk melted faster than the ice in my glass. The talk, as it usually is among the survivors of a New York party, was political. I could have made a contribution to it—for had I not talked with Mr. Adlai Stevenson a few nights before?—but felt no inclination even to show off. The people themselves were not boring, but their talk was. The topics were threadbare, the treatment of them routine. We were all parrots in a cage, wondering where the tropics had got to. There was no fire, no heart, in the talk. Round and round it went—what Ike might venture to do—what Senator This might say to Senator That—and people droned on, chiefly because they hated to break up the party and face the sleety night.

I told myself—and at the end of a party I really do tell myself things—that the political situation there in America was for once almost exactly like ours in Britain. Like Labour and the Tories, the Democrats and Republicans were nearly evenly matched, with some difference between their respective extremists, but little or none between the solid centres. On the domestic front, at least, no great burning issues divided people. But because we have conditioned ourselves to read about politics, to talk about politics, we continued reading and talking when there was hardly anything worth reading and talking about. (I am still addressing myself, covered with tobacco ash and slumped down in an armchair sixteen storeys above 57th Street.) And if we had any sense, in London or New York, either we would stop reading and talking about politics, as people have often done in the past, or we would make an effort to wake out of our sleep-walking and try to see our situation in a new light. We need not spend our lives at the fag-end of a party.

Even in international affairs, though everybody concerned in them might still be running round in a rat race, there were, I thought, signs of this staleness. The night before we had attended a concert given in the great hall of the United Nations Building. It was to celebrate the sixth anniversary of the Declaration of Human Rights, but it was not these Rights (though I believe in them) that had taken me there, but the thought of listening in comfort to the Boston Symphony under Charles Munch. We had Harty's arrangement of Handel's Water Music, some delicious Richard Strauss songs by a large smiling Viennese soprano, and, to conclude, the best performance of Berlioz' Fantastic Symphony I ever heard or ever hope to hear on this earth. The playing was of a kind to make the hair stand on end: here was the whole Romantic Movement, at once idiotic and glorious, furiously alive to the last glitter of the loved one's tears, the final mutter of doom. What a noble creature Western Man is when he reveals himself as a hundred-headed instrumentalist! This is the unity that should be in the United Nations.

Alas—alas—between Strauss and Berlioz—there was an address on these Human Rights, written by one U.N. high functionary and delivered into the microphone (the whole occasion was being broadcast) by another. And I longed to seize that microphone and to speak some real words into it. What we heard were dead thoughts in dead language. So might bees and ants have talked, already fixed in the pattern that would not be broken for millions of years. On an ordinary occasion in that hall, such thought, such language, might have passed unnoticed, but against the moving tracery and delicate fire of the music they were like two corpses on a dance floor. It was plain to be heard that all was make-believe, that no real men had any real rights, that probably at that very moment all manner of officials, throughout the world, were complacently ignoring all such rights and wrecking people's lives without a flicker of compunction.

I did not blame the two officers of the U.N., who had probably done their best in what was not their native language. They had lived and worked too long in a fatal atmosphere, in which harsh and intolerable things are covered with a blanket of woolly and almost meaningless language, in which *Human* does not mean human and *Rights* do not mean rights. Here everybody can agree that men have a right to health, education, well-paid regular work, excellent housing, and no doubt lovely obedient children and cabinet-size television sets, because it is all unreal, and nobody in genuine authority is prepared to guarantee that men should enjoy even their few essential rights, those rights against tyrannical government and its overbearing officials that our 'Free World' has been kick-

ing to bits for years. If a declaration of Human Rights has
to be celebrated while I am around, then let us have not
only the Boston Symphony—and I am all for that—but
also, instead of a lot of dingy wool, a statement giving the
names and addresses of all the people who, that night, have
been allowed to live their own lives in their own way again,
together with some apologies from the chief inquisitors.
That would be something to celebrate. I will offer odds of
ten-to-one, to be paid after death duties, that my own
modest funeral rites will be celebrated first.

As the party talk went on and on—what Knowland was
supposed to have said to Watkins and so forth—the same
sweepings of the political smoke-room that we get here—I
asked myself what we ought to be talking about, if only to
escape boring ourselves to death. Had everything been
settled then except for this dreary muddle of conflicting
personalities? Like hell it had! Certainly, with so much
rearmanent taking up the slack, on the whole we could say
that employment, hours, wages, general conditions, were
fairly good on both sides of the Atlantic, and that few
economists were uttering their usual grave warnings.
Money was being poured into the Christmas shops by the
sackful. The faces of the workers, sharply illuminated by
their television sets, were tranquil, if not downright blank.
The powerful, the rich, were not screaming for the police.
In the advertisements the automobiles now had "The
$100 Million Look!" Mr. Gilbert Harding was withdraw-
ing temporarily from *What's My Line?* and Alec Bedser's
form in Australia was still doubtful, but otherwise, Britain
stood firm. Nevertheless, there might be a few things
worth discussing, especially after a few Scotches.

97

Indeed, it might be that, like an audience at a show of conjuring, we were the victims of a misdirection of our attention. While we still concentrated on the rapidly diminishing differences between Capital and Labour, the Conservative and the Progressive, staring at them much as our grandfathers did, perhaps our whole society was changing so quickly, all round us, that we were still talking about one world while already living in another, quite different. Outside the political speeches, leading articles, and chatter, it was beginning to look like a society of Bossmen and Massmen, with neither of them caring a rap about anything we late-night talkers might say or do. Well, they could probably do without us. Yet we could fairly say that the look-out for a society seemed rather dubious, for the Bossmen are too busy settling their immediate problems of power to think far ahead, and Massmen hope not to have to think at all. Moreover, as several psychologists have been pointing out lately, men in a mass, as distinct from a genuine integrating group, are very dangerously situated, feeling the loss of many primary satisfactions and a growing sense of frustration. There may soon come a time when there are not enough new playthings to divert all these frustrated people. Then the lid might blow off.

I reminded myself that the economic phase of politics had a beginning not so very long ago, and that now we may be within sight of the end of it. Already it is the turn of the psychologist or social philosopher to utter the grave warnings. Soon it may be his turn to shape the policy of a new kind of party—that is, if everybody capable of joining it is not crushed out of existence between the Bossmen, of all colours, and the Massmen—a party that asks where we are going, and why, and is against sleep-walking and the routine acceptance of more-and-more-of-what-we-already-dislike. The quarrel then might not be about the owner-ship and control of the factory but about its very existence. This party would ask questions much earlier than present political parties do. It would examine and check what are now so many blind trends, acting on behalf of men's dignity, happiness, and possibilities of development. Life-haters would be denounced for bullying and bouncing us into accepting what we know in our hearts we do not want. But then, when I say 'us' I mean a dwindling minority, neither Massmen, who do not know what they want until they are told, nor Bossmen, who enjoy the bullying and bouncing.

Moreover, this minority stands on a shrinking platform. Twenty years ago, if I had had an article that expressed as frankly what I felt then as this expresses what I feel now, I could have offered it to one of a dozen papers, many of them with very large circulations, any one of which would have gladly printed it. And now? I do not pause to reply but to take a firmer grasp on these columns. There is just room to breathe in the space between Bossmen and Mass-men. However, we are still at liberty and no microphones have been installed yet in our sitting-rooms, so let us talk while we can—not about the largely artificial world in which Bossmen tinted blue or pink are imagined to be at one another's throats and Massmen, hating the least effort, are supposed to be alert and vigorous guardians of free-dom; but about the world that never gets into the papers, being so busy publishing them and swallowing them.

"Er——" I began, after telling myself all these things. But then somebody remembered a very good crack about Ike, just as the same sort of people here remember stories about Winston or Nye. Give us a little more time, and we will have Iked, Winstoned and Nyed ourselves into some sort of air-conditioned ant-hill.

THE NEW DROLLS

Ever since I used to sit, as a lad, in the fourpenny balcony of the Empire, Bradford (which was known in the profession as the 'comedians' grave'), I have been a collector and connoisseur of drolls, clowns, zanies. About thirty years ago I contributed a series of studies and appreciations of comedians to what was then a very stately morning paper. (It was I, in these columns, who wrote a tribute to Sid Field.) But the comedians I described in the middle 'twenties, unlike the star performers of today, had reached the top only after years of either concert-party work or provincial music-hall tours. The old music-halls were a matchless training ground. The fellows we watched from that fourpenny balcony (and there was a twopenny gallery behind us), as we sat on benches about six inches wide, packed closely together by experts at the job, had to be good—or God help them. Night after night, year after year, the old comedians worked away, getting an instant grip on those tough critical audiences, bringing their acts nearer and nearer to perfection. Just as a lion-tamer must have at least one lion, so a performer must have an audience, there in front of him; an act cannot be perfected except in the constant presence of a paying public, preferably from the North, where they want their money's worth.

Now the new droll who has natural ability and a genuine odd personality goes whizzing up to stardom in a few years. One really successful TV or radio series can put him up there. Then he will be paid hundreds of pounds a week to appear on the stage, not necessarily because he is thought to be funnier on the stage than on the air (though he should be), but because managers know that hundreds of thousands of his B.B.C. fans will want to see him in person. The result is that our most successful light entertainment is now dominated by these new stars from the B.B.C. who have risen since the war. So let us take a look at some of them, bearing in mind that these men are now important public figures. Humour is a very personal taste; but I will try, as if still endeavouring to please the examiners of my youth, to give reasons for my choice.

Jimmy Edwards has been extremely successful, both on the air and on the stage. He is fortunate in having a radio programme, written by two excellent wits, that provides him with some good foils and is economic in its use of material. (The nightmare of radio comedy is its appalling consumption of material.) He is a bustling, larger-than-life comedian, with an engaging informal style on the stage, an air of doing charades for us; never suggesting an actor, but rather a certain type of schoolmaster one used to know, the type that in anger would threaten to go out of its mind; and Jim, one may say, has done it and gone. Frankie Howerd, who is much funnier on the stage than he is in radio, is best as a kind of desperately worried zany, who arrives to do something he never gets done, just because he is suspicious of the management, the other performers, and wonders how soon he can get rid of the astonishingly stolid lady at the piano. There is about him almost a feminine fussiness; he reminds us of some despairing hostesses. He does not need witty material. Either you find his stage personality very funny itself, as I do, or do not like him at all.

Another despairing but different type is Tony Hancock, a very clever performer, owing more to art than to nature. He comes on all smiles and confidence, to recite, to sing, to dance, but is quickly reduced by the malice of circumstance, aided by a strange blank stooge who is the very image of no enthusiasm, to a gasping, pitiable wreck, his gleaming, rolling eye pleading for our tolerance, for just another chance. This is all in a high tradition of clowning. Good clowns never try to be funny; they are very serious but eager and hopeful creatures lost in a hostile world; and with great clowns like Grock and W. C. Fields the very furniture is menacing, never to be trusted. Al Read, who was an amateur a few years ago, has shot up like a rocket; he is, however, not a clown proper, a droll, but an extremely effective, self-taught character actor, whose work is based on very acute observation of Lancashire types, especially the loud, self-important chaps. He does not need the stage, as most of the others do, to reveal himself at his best.

Max Bygraves is a large, smooth, young man, dressy and faintly spivvy, but with an easy, relaxed manner that has charm. But whenever I have seen him I have always felt that he was better, or potentially better, than his material allowed him to be. He is like a cocktail that still needs a touch of Pernod or lemon juice or something to complete it. Last—for I have no space here for more than one other—is Norman Wisdom, still very young, who is perhaps the most successful so far with the big public. To be fair, I must explain that I have not seen him perform very recently. But when I did see him—and he was already a star then—I thought he had the appearance and feeling to be a Chaplinesque pathetic little clown, but that he had obviously been rushed to the top far too quickly, before he had mastered the all-important art of timing, in which the good clown must have an exquisite precision. Chaplin is a master of it. So was Grock. You may know in advance, as I did with Grock, exactly what a great clown is going to do or what will happen to him, yet so wonderful is his timing that you are as much taken by surprise as he appears to be. Norman Wisdom has not yet achieved this art, which demands years and years of careful study. It is best, too, if during those years the audience are not too friendly, too easily amused. The worst audience for a comedian trying to improve his act is the privileged invited studio audience, there to applaud anything and everything. A wet Monday in Leeds or Glasgow during a trade slump is what the ambitious and conscientious comedian should appreciate.

This rapid but slightly dubious progress leaves the new star droll facing many awkward questions. And do not imagine that he is such a gay, careless fellow, so busy enjoying his fabulous salary, that he neither knows nor cares how searching these questions are. Nearly all comedians of star quality are in fact extremely anxious and very conscientious performers, more aware of life and its pitfalls than most of their colleagues are, mere butterflies like singers. After all, the basis of good clowning is the contrast between the ideal and real, the expected and the actual, the shining dream and the grim businesses. So the new star drolls begin to worry about the division of their time between stage and air, the risk of using inferior material on the air or the further risk of using up good material, always hard to find, too quickly, the danger of losing the TV or radio public to competitors, the chance of remaining on the stage until an act is perfected. Finally, because his rise has been so rapid, he cannot help wondering if he is really good or has merely been lucky. He has come up quickly, he can go down quickly, too. The older comedians arrived the hard way, but once they were there they felt more secure. They could also save money, hardly possible now with our punitive taxation.

In my capacity as a collector and connoisseur, I try to visit most of the so-called revues (a name that should be reserved for less spectacular and more intimate entertainments) that frame the best of these new drolls. When I do, I admire such talent and art as they offer me, note with respect the ever-increasing precision of the chorus girls, who are far better on the stage, if not as trainees for the peerage, than those of my youth, and the recent marked improvement in *décor*, often borrowed from the masters of it, the French; but I hardly ever fail to be annoyed by the astonishing and really disgraceful lack of originality and ideas in these shows. Why have they, with so much money at their disposal, to be so corny? There are sketches that are more or less those I was beginning to yawn at in 1911. Why must they fall back, time after time, on scenes, situations, ideas that were flogged to death years ago? It is as if the new comedians had to take part in some time-honoured ritual of show business. There are religions that have changed faster than these entertainments. Soon they will be fixed for ever, like Punch-and-Judy.

After all, it is not this stale stuff that brings in the audience. The famous drolls are the attraction. Take out their names and personalities, and the shows die at once. But the crowds that make haste to see them have not made it a condition of their patronage that the shows must be entirely free from originality, topicality, ideas, genuine satire, real reference to our common lives. So long as their favourites are on the stage, not only could these audiences take something better than they are offered, but would probably welcome a little originality, a few ideas. The clowns and drolls could dissolve into laughter much that is bitterly frustrating now. Given some acceptable ideas to work with, they could do an even greater public service than they do already. And in this respect we are worse off than almost any other country I know. Are our drolls themselves afraid of richer and more original material? (And what a wonderful tragic clown has been wasted in Bud Flanagan!) Possibly; though I think they could be persuaded to try it; they are anything but stupid men. The fault lies with the managers. They will tell us that they use the best material available, but will not add that it is only the best within the very narrow field to which they limit themselves. Could some of my colleagues in the League of Dramatists provide better material, some originality, some ideas? Yes, I believe they could and that they ought to try. Across what is now the dramatists' desert, into which the star actors, either playing Shakespeare or filming, have disappeared, they must join hands with the drolls to make the big public laugh at itself.

DOERS AND SEERS

In Texas, where I was last autumn, there are some men who by successful 'wildcatting' and gambling in oil have piled up fortunes of hundreds of millions of dollars. They buy up newspapers and periodicals, put out radio and TV programmes that spread their prejudices across the States, and arrange for biographies to be written and for hundreds of thousands of copies to be bought and distributed. They feel they are wiser, nearer the 'good Lord' of whom they often speak, than ordinary men who would not know how to find a couple of hundred million dollars. The mantles of the Prophets have fallen upon them. The people should hearken unto them. And many of the people do, so that good men and women are hounded out of jobs, and ignorance, stupidity, monstrous prejudice, all darken the air.

It is clearly absurd that a man should think he is a sage and prophet because he has taken great wealth out of holes in the ground. But can we afford to smile at this notion? I doubt it. One reason why I went to Texas is that it offers us the spectacle of our contemporary society with the lid off, so to speak, and in Technicolor. When these dangerous donkeys say in effect "Money is power, power is wisdom", we cannot afford to smile at their naïveté, if only because the world we live in, the one that shapes and colours our lives, acts more or less on the same belief. It is a world that has come to imagine, with disastrous consequences, that the doer is also the seer.

Stated baldly like this, it is obviously nonsense. The doer and the seer are quite different—are indeed opposing —types of men. One has to be in the thick of it, the other must remain detached. One acts, the other looks on. One mind is geared for quick decisions, the other is slow, brooding, comprehensive. Nobody in his senses would expect a born seer to *do*. That much is generally acknowledged. But it is equally ridiculous to suppose that a dashing and triumphant doer can really *see*. And this is by no means generally acknowledged. It may be in theory, but it is not in actual practice. We live in fact in a world of doers who also ask us—or compel us—to regard them as seers. And the mess they are making stains the pages of every newspaper we read.

In the records of the ancient world, especially those of the East, we read how emperors and conquerors, whose mere frown could mean death, were visited by sages and prophets who told them plainly to their faces that they did not know what they were doing. It was assumed then, even by the masters of power, that power and wisdom were not the same thing, that there existed another realm in which armies meant nothing, that deep insight could not be hacked out with a sword. Any man acting on that assumption now would probably soon find himself either in jail or in a mental hospital. Indeed, those who enjoy power make more and more moves to protect themselves from any adverse criticism. In this they have been immensely helped by the hysterical atmosphere of our bomb-heavy world. Even if the bombs should be outlawed, this atmosphere will remain, to complete its task of turning people into sheep.

There is just a chance that a man might inherit power and still retain some characteristics of the seer. But a man who has spent most of his adult life intriguing, bargaining, fighting for power will have rid himself of these characteristics, if he had any, very early in the grim game. There would be no harm in this if, while on the way up, he did not convince himself that with power comes wisdom. But if wisdom does not come from million-dollar holes in the ground, why should it come with a majority of the votes, the secretaryship of the Party, a control of the army and navy, or whatever else puts a man in supreme authority? Somewhere in the vast territory controlled by Stalin, for example, there must have been a few sages, perhaps tucked away in Central Asian monasteries, who were much wiser than he was. Did he send for them, as many a despot of the ancient world did? I cannot swear he didn't, but the odds are heavily against it. Did he need a seer in the midst of all his doing? In my view, he needed one very badly. He had cunning but no real insight.

Chinese leaders as great as Mao and Chou En-lai could bring themselves, long ago, to stand abashed before smiling, slit-eyed old mystics who commanded nobody and owned nothing. But our despots are both too narrow-minded and too conceited. They are where they have always wanted to be, on top of the heap. How could anyone be wiser than they are? If a few old deviationists look like giving trouble, shoot them, torture them, offer them a choice of solitary confinement or brain-washing. Don't try to improve your own mind and outlook; simply get rid of everybody and everything that might improve them: that is the new style, headlong in pursuit of catastrophe.

No doubt it is all much better on our side of the Curtain, where perhaps our great doers consult—of course in secret —such seers as they can discover. But there are times even here when it is difficult not to feel rather dubious. It may be necessary—I do not propose to argue the point here— that we in England should manufacture hydrogen bombs. But even the most enthusiastic admirer of potential large explosions would have to admit there is no medicine here for a sick civilisation. All we have here is a bit more frantic doing. But who among these doers, whose wisdom we are asked to admire, is *seeing* anything he did not see before? Who is telling us what is wrong with Man, not what is wrong with another set of people in another part of the world, with this policy and that policy, but what is wrong with *us*? There are two great questions. The first is —how do we get out of this hydrogen-bomb-world without being blown out of it? The second is—how do we begin to live so that we do not pile up these frustrations and resentments? I do not blame a man for not knowing the answers. But he must not ask me to admire his superior insight, his statesmanlike wisdom. He must not pretend that the doer is all-sufficient, that the seer is no longer necessary.

Even if we descend from these supreme heights of in- effectuality, where *Don't Know* is in conference with *Can't Imagine*, we can observe this fatal notion, that wisdom comes with power, hard at work. Most of us have relatives, friends, acquaintances, who have been determined for years to arrive somewhere important, to be on top some- how, to achieve power. Their lives have been conditioned by this determination. They have allowed themselves to think about nothing else. No detachment is possible to them, otherwise a move or two, a trick or two, might be lost. Feverishly they search for the next ladder, try to avoid the next snake. They run from committee to committee, with something that might be useful on each agenda. They join forces with Smith; they drop Robinson; they make overtures to Jones. They are on the telephone from eight one morning until two the next. They neglect their wives and children, forget their friends. They no longer read, enjoy music or the theatre, take walks, talk affectionate nonsense, consider the great mysteries of this life. In them the lover, poet, philosopher, friend, all wither away. Everybody and everything become mere means to an end. Ambition eats them away. And as it is power of some sort they want, it is power they achieve.

It is at this point, when they have the power, the mischief begins. If they realised how much they had lost on the way up, if they knew themselves to be psychologically lop-sided and spiritually maimed, no harm would be done. We need these strenuous and single-minded doers. But now, when they have the power, they should consult the seers to learn what use they should make of it. And this is what they will not do. They can hardly be blamed. They have succeeded in a world which sees itself in terms of power, which regards the power-seeker as the typical superior man, which hardly acknowledges the existence of the seer. Why should the triumphant doer consult anybody—except perhaps other triumphant doers—when he has arrived where every sane, vigorous, able, ambitious man would like to be? If the seer had these essential qualities, he too would be in a position of authority. Why ask the advice of a man who does not even know how to look after himself? Does success consult failure? This is what the multi-millionaire oilmen would say. Some of the men much nearer to us than these Texan toughs, our own smoother types, might not say it; but they would think it.

If this supremacy of the doer were only concerned with manufacturing pins or selling shoes, no great harm would be done. But he shoulders his way to the top not only in business, politics, administration, but also in many forms of education and in every kind of mass communication. Everything now is so big and elaborate that only a ruthless doer can cope with it. But once he has coped with it, then he feels that it should express him and his type and not any vague, woolly-minded chap who drifts along. If the seer gets in at all, it will only be at a very low level, where he cannot do much harm. And if he decides to ignore all this massive thundering machinery of communication, he will discover that his tiny dwindling audience can hardly hear him. The voices that can be heard everywhere, from which indeed it is hard to escape, belong to doers-in-chief, all the camp followers of power, and doers hastily rigged out to look like seers. (For example, American big business parsons who run large churches, TV and radio pro-grammes, advice bureaux, and turn out syndicated columns and best-sellers.) These disguises and deceptions are oc-casionally necessary simply because the great simple public, for which they are always intended, has not entirely lost touch with the ancient world and still has a lingering belief in disinterested wise men, sages, seers. And perhaps the dupes know more than those who deceive them.

A NOTE
ON BILLY GRAHAM

When I was in America last autumn, many people asked
me about Billy Graham's campaign in England, about
which they had read the most astonishing reports. Not all
of them were opposed to his fundamental evangelism—
indeed, one or two of the Texans believed in it—but all
were surprised that the cool and fairly hard-headed
British, three thousand miles away from the Bible Belt,
should have contributed to this triumph. I could only
reply that I had not seen or heard Billy Graham myself,
that the reports seemed to me vastly exaggerated, but that
I did not believe that the post-war British were as cool and
hard-headed as Americans thought they were. I also
pointed out that while Billy Graham did appear to have
overcome a good deal of initial prejudice, he seemed to be
the essential part of a publicity organisation really formidable in its power and smooth working, a jet engine of
public relations. And this, by the way, much that I read
and heard in America amply confirmed. Billy did his stuff
all right—but—man, what a set-up!

Now, thanks to television, an intimate searching
medium, I have looked at and listened to Billy Graham
at closer range, throughout a long sermon, than most of
his admirers have. (Unless of course they too were in front
of their TV sets on Good Friday). Unlike some of my

fellow-viewers here, a mixed company for Easter week-end, I did not find him personally disagreeable. Nor did he seem particularly attractive. He did not strike me as being in any way insincere; on the other hand, I felt no conviction of a burning sincerity, of that fire in the belly which made some of the wilder nonconformist parsons of my youth appear almost incandescent. He preached the same old bible-thumping stuff. I will say nothing about his theology, if only because it is to my mind at once incredible and repulsive, except to remark that I could find nothing new in it. Its like can be found on any Sunday morning in any Little Bethel. And though he was fluent and had a nice sense of timing, he was no blazing, thundering orator, like some of the old evangelists I remember, especially the spell-binders from Wales. What distinguished him were his appearance and manner. Instead of looking and behaving like a minor prophet, straight from the desert or the savage hills, he looked and behaved like a rather excited successful young American business-man, like one of those well-groomed fellows who sit at tables in the Chase National Bank or the Guaranty Trust, called upon to explain, with some vigour, why collateral will be necessary if you expect a loan.

I admit, however, that this is an important difference. For we all are tied to America these days, unless we are Iron Curtainers. America calls the tune we all dance to, in every possible sense of that expression. Whatever our contemporary age has, America has the most of. It is the jackpot country. If we are safely bound for an earthly paradise, the Americans will be there first. If we are all going to Hell, they will also be there first. Even the atom and hydrogen bombs had to come from America. But now, out of America, looking like a typical clean young American who drinks his orange juice and coffee, eats his cereal and waffles, drives in a big, fast car to play golf, is the bearer of the Word. Salvation has come, as it should, from America. Our sins are being denounced in an American accent. Heaven is being promised again by a figure who might easily have a five-year contract with M.-G.-M. Coca-Cola and cornflakes have been magically transformed into the bread and the wine. Out of General Motors and United Steel have come Original Sin and Redemption. Yes, this is a very important difference. But it does not explain the whole story.

Many years ago—and I confess to having forgotten the date—another celebrated American evangelist came to this country. This was Aimée Semple Macpherson. She was a very different character from Billy Graham, and her methods were entirely opposed to his, being blatantly theatrical, brash to the point of impudence, sexy as a touring revue. Nevertheless, she preached more or less the same doctrine, taking its stand on whatever the Good Book says. But she was a flop. The Albert Hall, which can take anything but angels from Los Angeles, was the scene of her Waterloo. True, her methods were unsuitable to a colder climate. True, Aimée was not a girl who could be enthusiastically sponsored by Bishops, Members of Parliament, editors, at least in public. But I do not think this is enough to explain the difference between almost complete failure and an astonishing triumph. There are two other reasons, much more important, and they are interconnected.

In the first place, Mrs. Macpherson's publicity was childish compared with Billy Graham's. It is like comparing two or three advance men working for a circus with the public relations machinery of a great corporation or a political party. (If this seems an exaggeration, I refer the reader to the article in *Time*—by no means hostile—that gave a glimpse of the methods of the Billy Graham organisation). During the last twenty-five years we have advanced further and further into the age of propaganda, elaborately planned and organised publicity, high-pressure advertisement, public relations on every possible scale. What was once rough-and-ready ballyhoo, the old Barnum stuff, is now the patient work of a trained staff, able to exploit every device to capture public attention and interest. A Billy Graham no more lands here at a moment's notice, hoping for the best, than a General Eisenhower lands in France at a moment's notice, hoping for the best: both arrivals have come at the end of months and months of careful planning, staff work, campaigns by all manner of instructed teams. Little that can be done ahead is left to chance. Nevertheless, the evangelist, unlike the general, still has the incalculable public mind to contend with. It might still turn against him, even if the softening-up process has been carried as far as it will go. The British might still close their minds and harden their hearts. Billy could be a flop, as poor Aimée was. It depends how the British are feeling.

This brings us to the second reason for Billy's triumph here. He arrived at the right time, like the other conquering William. Let us concede that among his vast audiences there are some people who have been longing for his particular brand of Salvation and are genuinely converted by him. But these appear to be a tiny minority. After all, on Good Friday night he made a long and fairly emotional appeal to what must have been one of his largest audiences, packing the Kelvin Hall, and yet at the end, when he asked people to come forward if they wanted to make sure that night of going to Heaven, promising them, too, that it could all be done with a minimum of inconvenience and embarrassment, almost like a man arranging a de luxe tour, he had no great rush of converts. Possibly some hundreds may have drifted up, rather as people emerge from a music-hall audience to assist a conjurer; but no wet-faced mob, already feeling the flames of hell behind them, stormed the rostrum. If, as we are told, all the other thousands there were 'hungering for religion', they remained curiously deaf and blank to the entreaties of this new prophet. Gone were the frenzied scenes that took place every night in the tents of the old evangelists. If Billy is different, looking like a young business-man, so is the audience, looking like an enormous meeting not of sinners but of shareholders. This may be the new revival atmosphere, religion in the electronic age, but I feel if sin is to be washed away, in the old evangelical style not entirely abandoned, then far more blood, sweat and tears will be needed.

Coming to the point—and it is the point of this Note— I do not believe that Billy Graham has been such a spectacular success because the British now hunger for religion. (I wish they did.) It is because what so many of us want now is a show, a show that has been written up in the Press, a show that is linked to radio and TV. Aimée

Semple Macpherson failed because her personality and methods were dubious, her publicity crude and inadequate. But there was another reason. The people she hoped to dominate and enchant still had things to think about; they had worries and problems; they had political passions and enthusiasms; they were not then completely under the spell of mass communications. Times have changed, and with them a large mass of the people. Many of the post-war British now live from one show to the next, at the mercy of mass communications, which tell them what to expect to bring Wednesday week to life. There is a vacuum that must be filled. Politics, to exist for them at all, must be a show. Patriotism is a show with an expensive regal cast. Sport is a show. The arts are a show on ice. And now, with the arrival of the stream-lined Billy Graham organisation, elaborately geared to the new tempo, religion is a show. I am not doubting Billy Graham's personal sincerity—I am sure he believes what he says and is simply doing what he feels to be his duty— but he himself would hardly deny that he is a showman too, and the central figure of a massive show organisation. And he brought a show to the very people who wanted a show. And I am afraid that it is about all most of them do want.

Now we need only find an answer to one more question. Why has Billy Graham had a more immediate and dramatic success here in Britain than he ever had at home? I have already suggested one reason—the fact that he comes from America. But there is another, more important. It will surprise many readers, who must accept my assurance that I do not write without evidence. The truth is that

now the British crowd is more easily enticed and dominated by mass communications, showmanship, ballyhoo,
than the American crowd is. The Americans have had a
great deal more of it, and for years were far more respon-
sive to it, but while there is in them still a strain of the
gullible and hysterical, there is also, the work of a powerful
antibody, a strain of the sceptical, the cynical, the sardonic. The satirical journalist and the jeering comic are
figures of power in America. Poisons may multiply but so
do the antidotes in that land of productivity. But the
newly arrived British bring with them into this world of
mass communications, shows, and ballyhoo a certain
innocence, belonging to an earlier age, leaving them un-
protected by any rough popular cynicism. They are
bowled over by the new nonsense as easily as the Martian
invaders, in Wells's story, fell victims to the strange
bacteria of this world. Their minds are wide open as well
as being empty. Today it is Billy Graham, old-fashioned
fundamental evangelism plus planned public relations and
electronics: no great harm, no great good; mostly, just
another show. But tomorrow—who?—what? This Note
sounds a caution.

OUR NEW SOCIETY

Mr. Gaitskell, my morning paper tells me, has perceived a new trend in our society, and he says of it: "Call it, if you like, a growing Americanisation of outlook." Some of us were publicly noting this trend over ten years ago, but I for one never found any Labour politician who thought it worth discussing. Their minds were on more serious things. Now, of course, it is different. In the same way, since the general election, sensible public men have told me, rather hesitantly, cautiously, that some apathy about politics seems to exist and that perhaps industrial man's state of mind may have something to do with these expensive strikes. I sometimes think the basis of a sound, sensible public career and reputation is simply to have control of an unusual amount of bland impudence, so that, staring at him hard, you can solemnly tell a man a part of what he has been telling you for years.

Mr. Gaitskell, who has just discovered a growing Americanisation of outlook that may profoundly affect the future of the Labour Party, is neither impudent nor stupid. The reason that he is years and years out of date, and that he is now telling us what we were trying to tell him even before the war ended, is that he does not appreciate the interdependence of things in this world. He sees himself as a serious man who must restrict his attention to serious matters, the sort of stuff that finds its way into the

City columns of *The Times*. It would never occur to him to take a look at *Mabel's Weekly* or *Filmfans Pictorial*. It is now some years since certain sections of the popular press, still pretending to be more British than the Union Jack, began to treat London as a suburb of New York. The theatre publicity of 1945 and the mood of the electorate in 1955 are linked together; the trouble is, so few people give both of them some thoughtful consideration. And it is from the frivolities and trivialities, far below the level of a public man's attention, that the little straws come, those straws that still show which way the wind is blowing. Now that this wind has arrived at gale force, serious dependable men, sound thinkers, notice at last that all the air is moving in one direction.

Nevertheless, to talk of "a growing Americanisation of outlook" will not do. It is years óut of date. We are living now in a new society. It would be unfair both to my distinguished collaborator and our joint publishers to quote from a book, called *Journey Down a Rainbow*, that will, I hope, appear in the autumn. But in my half of the book I coin a name for this new society. We must give it a name if only in order to stop calling it American. True, America is at the head of it. But the notion that this society only flourishes in America and is merely fleetingly reflected in Western Europe and elsewhere is, to my mind no longer acceptable. We are all in it. (That is, in a broad sense, as members of a contemporary society. As individuals here and there, we may still be more or less living in the eighteenth century, the Middle Ages, even the Stone Ages.) It is only fair to point out that some of the most active and severest critics of this new society are themselves American. In fact, the thoughtful American is more aware of the dangers and weaknesses than all but a very few Western Europeans. The American cannot help but realise that, for better or worse, he lives in this society. The European may fool himself, and generally does, into believing that its existence is still a mere distant threat. He is in a more dangerous situation—and this applies particularly to the English—just because he cannot or will not face the fact that the change has already occurred.

If our man is a public figure, it is ten to one that in his writings and speeches he still assumes the existence of a society that has in fact now ceased to exist. Clearly, this is a very dangerous illusion. It is as if a man imagined he was riding in a carriage-and-pair when he was already travelling at sixty miles an hour in a car, as if he still asked us to admire the glossy action of the horses, the coachman's skill with the whip, the sensible pace of ten miles an hour. Of course, if he is an intuitive, as many successful public men are, especially the officially Conservative types, he will actually behave as if the change had taken place— otherwise, where would he be?—but he will give us no sign that his thought accepts it. He will talk to us about our traditions, even if those traditions no longer have any inner validity and force and are in fact only part of the great show that amuses the idle-minded mob. He will still praise the love of liberty of people who would cheerfully exchange their last glimpses of freedom for a new car, a refrigerator, and a fourteen-inch television screen. He will congratulate the same people on their power of choice when he must know very well, for he has often been in conference with the experts, that now they have about as much real power of choice as the people called from the audience by a conjurer. He will orate about our Christian community to men and women who are living in the most blankly secular and material society the world has known since Hadrian's Rome. He will praise the spiritual values of people who would not spend ten shillings or an hour on them, who have believed for years that all they can hope for is a better spring mattress in the execution chamber.

A few weeks ago something happened in America that appeared to rouse no interest whatever in our popular papers. Three elderly judges announced that the State Department had no right to refuse passports to citizens without due process of law. These three judges belonged to the society that is rapidly vanishing. The State Department, which I suspect will continue to prevent citizens, convicted of no crime, from leaving the country, belongs to the new society. The Press that considered the decision of these judges not to be worth half a column also belongs to the new society. It knows what interests the mass of its readers, who, as members of the new society, care nothing if the State continues to exercise more and more power and the individual loses more and more essential liberty. We are often told that in our new society there is a new middle class taking the place of the old. And this is true if you think that attitudes of mind are of no importance, if you think in terms of income, rugs, baths, easy chairs, and household gadgets. But the old middle class, with all its faults, had two virtues. Being in the middle, above the level at which ham and eggs are more important than liberty, below the level at which the enjoyment of direct power becomes itself important, it was sharply suspicious of all concentrations of power and of all threats to liberty. Its second virtue was that, not being concerned with elementary security and not seeking the enjoyment of power, it was able to feel a certain sense of responsibility about society in general, often making some sacrifice to keep values alive. It said 'we' and not 'they'. But the new middle class in our new society, though no doubt crammed with nice people, well-behaved, clean and healthy and kind, does not possess these virtues. First, it wants security at almost any cost. Secondly, under the relentless pressure of mass communications and everything that manipulates them, it wants what it is told to want, accepting almost without question any shoddy cheapjack set of values. So more and more we find ourselves among either the simple or the cynical, the manipulators and the manipulated. The creative, enthusiastic, vigilant, and combative types, like the old Radicals I once knew, begin to look like anachronisms. Which is what they are in the new society.

In the most strangely prophetic poem of this century, Yeats began by declaring that things were falling apart and that the centre could not hold. The new society, which has no centre, was on its way to us. It is now all round us. (In my view, it embraces almost all the earth, because Communism only offers a grimmer variation of this society, with propaganda and the secret police taking the place of high-pressure advertising and salesmanship. It has the same pattern of rulers and ruled, the actively powerful and the passively powerless, and what it wants is more or less the same.) And here in England we must not deceive ourselves, because Derby still looks different from Dallas. If Derby had the money, space, and energy, it would soon look like Dallas: it is on the way there. That is why it is too late now to refer to "a growing Americanisation of outlook". In the last piece I contributed to these columns, on Billy Graham, I suggested that now we might be worse off than the Americans, and it seems to be significant that most of the letters I received, agreeing with my estimate of Billy Graham's campaign, arrived from America. There is at least less self-deception over there, more signs of a definite revolt. I find one odd bit of evidence in the way in which the death and personality of Dylan Thomas impressed the American imagination. For here, to the point of self-destruction perhaps, was an unabashed and loud-voiced rebel against every possible standard of the new society, a Celtic bard among the skyscrapers, a man who refused to be conditioned like the air he finally breathed. And it was the American crowd, not the British (still being told that a new TV parlour game is a national event), who, for a little space, with their ancestors stirring in the remoter depths of their minds, contemplated the doomed figure of this archetypal poet with strange mixed feelings, bewilderment, regret, and awe.

It must be all of fifteen years since I wrote a little piece for *Horizon* called 'Labour Leaders At The Ivy', in which I asked myself if they had any guiding vision of the kind of Britain they hoped to create when they achieved power. I suspected then, and know now, they had not. Old hands who for years had used perorations about William Morris and Merrie England helped to contrive an England in which artists faced starvation and City men walked away with millions. Now, after a sharp defeat that could easily

125

have been anticipated, one of the younger and more astute of them has arrived at a recognition of "a growing Americanisation of outlook". But it is something more than an imported outlook he and his friends must consider now. It is indeed a whole new society, much further removed from 1900 than 1900 was from 1850. We are always being told about visitors from some other planet. They have arrived, and may be found in the nearest street. They are the children of a new age.

CANDLES
BURNING LOW

In our new society there is a growing dislike of original, creative men. The manipulated do not understand them; the manipulators fear them. The tidy committee men regard them with horror, knowing that no pigeonholes can be found for them. We could do with a few original, creative men in our political life—if only to create some enthusiasm, release some energy—but where are they? We are asked to choose between various shades of the negative. The engine is falling to pieces while the joint owners of the car argue whether the footbrake or the handbrake should be applied. Notice how the cold, colourless men, without ideas and with no other passion but a craving for success, get on in this society, capturing one plum after another and taking the juice and taste out of them. Sometimes you might think the machines we worship make all the chief appointments, promoting the human beings who seem closest to them. Between midnight and dawn, when sleep will not come and all the old wounds begin to ache, I often have a nightmare vision of a future world in which there are billions of people, all numbered and registered, with not a gleam of genius anywhere, not an original mind, a rich personality, on the whole packed globe. The twin ideals of our time, organisation and quantity, will have won for ever.

The more sinister fairy-tales are probably true. Wishes are magically granted, but then the people live unhappily ever after. They wanted the wrong things, or things in the wrong order. Just as people now demand a smoothly cemented walk and then wonder where the flowers have gone. We should like to have some towering geniuses, to reveal us to ourselves in colour and fire, but of course they would have to fit into the pattern of our society and be ready to take orders from sound administrative types. We have cultural departments, with files already allotted to various types of genius; we have colossal fuss-making mechanisms, served by armies of public-relations men, commentators, and gossipers; but genius itself, the authentic flame, seems shy of the crowded and noisy scene. But perhaps it is the hidden wish, the secret desire, that sets in motion the magic. And perhaps our society does not really want great talent, genius, the flame.

These thoughts arose from the fact that, as I write this, the main theatrical topic here, in London, is the *décor* of the new production of *King Lear* by a Stratford company headed by Sir John Gielgud. (And let it be clearly understood that I am not criticising Sir John, his producer Mr. George Devine, and their associates. They are outside the argument.) This *décor*, I believe, is the work of a Japanese artist living in America. The production has already been taken to Holland, Switzerland, Austria. All this seems impressive, suggesting an international world of culture, a Theatre uniting the ends of the earth. Arts Councils, British Councils, have not toiled in vain. The harvest is near. There is hope for us yet. But how much? I dislike dimming any gleam of hope, to reveal a prospect bleaker than ever; but we must take a closer view.

It is not difficult to imagine all the fuss and palaver, all the administrating and organising, the cables, telegrams, telephone calls, letters, contracts, schedules, timetables, behind this particular production, which in turn is bringing into the world, already dizzy with news and gossip, whole acres, for which forests are being sacrificed, of newspaper and magazine comment and photographs, gush and sneers and backchat. And all this is typical of our new society, our age of administrators and organisers, time-table and schedule makers, journalists pretending to be critics, illiterates pretending to be journalists. What is also typical of our new society is that the only essentially creative thing here, the play itself, belongs to another age altogether, coming to us across three and a half centuries. A host of contemporaries are trying to light and warm themselves by the flame that once blazed in Shakespeare's mind. Here we might pause to reflect that the London of today, more than ten times the size of Shakespeare's, with ten times the number of theatres, has actually fewer dramatists of great talent. You can easily multiply people, machinery, fuss, but not talent and genius. In all that is essential to a vital Theatre, Elizabeth the First was more fortunate than Elizabeth the Second. But then the real Elizabethans genuinely wanted dramatic genius, so the magic worked for them. What we want are aeroplanes that break the sound barrier, and this is what we have been given.

If Shakespeare were alive today and offered us a *King Lear*, not only would Shaftesbury Avenue and Broadway tell him he was wasting his time turning out such stuff, but he might be in danger of being asked to see a psychiatrist. The only way we keep Shakespeare is by turning him into a cultural figure, which means that we need not take him seriously. A contemporary dramatist, caught in the mood in which *King Lear* was written, hot, black, and bitter, would be denounced by the more responsible Press as a menace, and savagely jeered at by the others as a lunatic. The creative flame has to be seen at a great distance, and even then through the smoked glasses of cultural history. The very people who boast they never miss a new production of *King Lear* would run in horror, as if the pavement were exploding, from a contemporary drama of the same quality. All the fuss about *décor* gives the game away. When the drama is burningly alive, compelling people to listen in horror, amazement, wonder, and joy, imposing a new vision of this life upon the audience, nobody cares what tights and whiskers the actors are wearing. A designer's Theatre is a Theatre in which the dramatists are dead or dying. Once plays are produced not because of what the dramatists are saying but to introduce a certain new shade of pink, the vital Theatre has gone, and any kind of Theatre is on its way out.

The new society organises—or tries to organise—the arts, just as it organises so many activities. If committees, memoranda, *In* and *Out* trays, general busybodying, gossip and palaver, could do the trick, we would make the Athens of Pericles, the Florence of the de Medicis, the London of Elizabeth and James the First, look like dingy suburbs. For sheer fuss, comment, gossip, about the arts, no previous society can compare with ours. We are ready to lay on culture like hot-and-cold water. As soon as anybody has created anything, it is black and crawling with all the types who are still waiting for somebody to create something. (And the fact that they are dependent upon a creative instinct they do not possess themselves makes them hostile to the creator.) And while the parasites multiply, the body that nourishes them is beginning to look emaciated. Not that there is any lack of artistic activity on a certain level. Never was there more. In schools throughout the land, painters and sculptors are teaching painters and sculptors to teach painters and sculptors to teach students who will become teachers of painting and sculpture: in an infinite regress of dimming visual culture. Never were there more publishers or more new books. All the wave-lengths hum with comment upon and discussion of the arts. Our society ought to be ablaze with genius. And if it is not, then perhaps it is because there are too few flames and far too many shades, snuffers, and extinguishers. There are too many foresters for too few trees.

For one reason and another, I happen to be fairly well acquainted with new fiction. Now the average level is high, much higher than when I started writing. Novelists 'of promise' are almost ten a penny. Of scores of these books, you cannot honestly say they are bad. Their writers do not make fools of themselves; they have read a good deal before they began to write; they all make an excellent beginning. Yet among all these novels, which have been piling up for years, where are the established novelists? Where are the writers so well known that they can be justly regarded as public figures? Where, in the Madame Tussaud's of the national consciousness, are the men of letters? Or, for that matter, the other kinds of creative artists? Name ten, widely known and highly regarded, under fifty years of age. Who and where are the massive talents, the towering personalities, the men of genius? Who represents us abroad as we ought to be represented—by the English mind blazing with art and throwing a light on the world we all share—and not by the assistant secretary to the Department of Drains, the vice-chairman of the Busybodies Association, the Secretary of the Society of Stuffed Shirts?

I shall be told that we are reaching the end of a cultural epoch, that this is inevitably an age of criticism and not creation. This sounds all right until you look round for the criticism, and then you realise that it is out of date, that we have passed this point, that we are beginning something new and not gracefully ending something old. True, we have criticism in quantity, but what about the quality? Where are the great figures, the definitive works? I do not say we have not still among us some critics well worth reading, men whose periodical work has a sparkle. But they all seem to be so short-winded; a sprint down a column tires them; not for them the big books, the wide surveys, the formidable judgments. Where are the fit companions of the creative giants? They were beginning to fade from the scene when I was young. No, this is not an age of criticism. It is the new age of snap personal judgments—*I like this, I don't like that*, of snippety comment, of art gossip and chatter, of newspaper twaddle about somebody's beard or boots. Because in its heart, if it has one, our new society is hostile to genius, to creation, to bold original minds. It knows these are dangerous to its designs.

The man with a passion, a flair, a creative zest, even for one of its own new media, is to be avoided, and there must be brought in, to control the medium, to let the blood out of it, some Machiavelli of governing boards, some Metternich of faked agenda and office intrigue, somebody who will never put a foot wrong nor a finger right. In this chilly atmosphere a creative, original man might as well be a rogue elephant. The flame of genius can find no fuel in it. So the flame pales and dwindles; the great voices, proclaiming our despair, our hope, our anger and our brotherhood, no longer reach us except from the past, do not speak for us in our present situation; and millions of innocent people, who have been told they are within sight of the promised land, wonder why they are not as happy as they ought to be. They wait for the truth that genius always proclaims, and some of them will have to wait a long time.

A PERSONAL NOTE

When readers agree with what I am saying here, they write to me to tell me so. (And so wide is the circulation of the *N.S. & N.* now, these letters arrive from many different parts of the world.) But when readers disagree with me, they do not write to me but to the paper. I cannot blame them, because this is what I do too, in my capacity as a reader. We readers are annoying creatures, just as we writers are misunderstood and long-suffering beings.

The time has come, however, when I must say something about myself—wilderness or no wilderness—if only to prevent critical readers, irritated by these pieces of mine (which incidentally should be regarded as polemical essays and not as reports by a research worker), from committing themselves to all manner of nonsense, and to check, if possible, the growth of a ridiculous legend. While this legend merely circulated in a section of the popular Press, which sees me, as I see it, as One of the Enemy, it could be ignored. But when it finds its way into these columns, it cannot remain unchallenged.

This legend runs as follows. There was once a Jolly Jack Priestley. But a weight of years, together with all the money he has accumulated, has sadly changed him. Now he is sour, without sympathy and generosity, just another rich ageing man, grumbling about his taxes, suspicious of the young, unable to adjust himself to social changes, convinced that the world is going to the bad. And I hereby declare, with all the emphasis at my command, that all this is rubbish, quite untrue to the facts.

In the first place, there never was a Jolly Jack. If jollity has to be dragged in, then all I can say is that both in my work and in my personal life I am in fact much jollier than I used to be. In the second place, I am nothing like as well off as I used to be, and lead a far less elaborate and pampered existence. In the third place, I regard the young with more sympathy than most men of my age do, and find it easier than they do to adapt myself to social changes, many of which I strongly advocated. Moreover, strange as it may seem to some minds, I try to examine the world not from the standpoint of self-interest but from that of a man, more fortunate than many others, who can afford to tell an unpleasant truth or two, not having a boss to please, a job to lose. This is one advantage of being a writer: you can venture, though not of course entirely without risk, to blurt out the truth now and again.

I may of course go badly wrong. About many things I hope I am wrong, and nobody will be more delighted than I would be to be proved wrong. (Whatever else I may be, I am certainly no hater of life.) But I am rather tired of being offered, by way of reply, simply so many personal attacks. These will not do. I know I pass in many quarters as a supremely touchy, aggressive fellow, ready to quarrel at the drop of a word. (This too I believe to be a legend, for I have actually conducted fewer quarrels than most writers, have kept my friends all my adult life, have had the same publishers, both here and in America, for thirty years.) But it is a fact that I dislike making personal attacks, doing everything I possibly can to avoid them. I denounce tendencies, mass movements, signs of the times, not persons. I believe other people can be *honestly wrong*. (The general absence of this belief is one of the evils of our time and does much to explain our suspicion, methods of persecution, shocking cruelty.) But instead of being given evidence to show that my thinking is faulty, my conclusions unsound, nine times out of ten all I am offered is this Jolly Jack rubbish, with a lot of doubts about my elementary good will and disinterestedness.

This is old stuff turned inside out. Many years ago, when I was denouncing mass unemployment and the dole system and giving some of the first detailed descriptions of the distressed areas, not only was I told that I was merely a sentimental story-teller unable to understand economic realities, but I was also told that I was taking this line to curry favour with the working classes, to sell more books and theatre seats. When one remembers the situation these people were in, without a hope of buying a book or a theatre seat, the blazing idiocy of such personal criticism is obvious. (Actually I lost some bookbuyers and play-goers, probably for ever.) But I do assure the reader that much recent criticism, now delivered from the other side, is just as idiotic. All I am doing now is what I was doing then—trying to tell the truth as I see it. I exaggerate of course, adopting shock tactics, but that is a fault of manner. There will always be a type of reader who is irritated by such a manner, who wants a leading article topic in a leading article style, and I do not blame such readers. But at least they might try not to confuse manner with matter.

For when readers announce they are tired of my railing against the Welfare State and taxation, I begin to feel that either I can't write or they can't read. I happen to believe that both the Welfare State, not because of the welfare but because of the State, and a tax system that penalises hard work and encourages gambling, have their dangers. But most of these "Thoughts in the Wilderness" have been about something quite different, about the poverty of creative ideas in our chief political parties, about the menace of block thinking, about the colossal impact of our mass communications, about the relation between a style of living and the atomic bomb, about the true significance of Billy Graham, and, above all, about all those rapid changes, not planned by anybody, that are compelling us, whether we recognise the fact or not, to live in a new society. Of course, I may exaggerate the importance of those changes, the difference between the new society and the old. Some allowance must be made for a man who cannot help dramatising every situation. I expect—and would welcome—correction by cooler heads. But it simply won't do to tell me either that I am merely repeating what disgruntled old men mutter in their clubs (I am doing nothing of the kind) or that I am crying "Woe—woe!" out of some private abyss of pessimism. The chief difference between me and most of my critical correspondents here is that while I remain a rebel, still hoping for and believing in something better for my children and grandchildren, they have turned themselves into smooth apologists, those 'official spokesmen' who are always being quoted at us.

If I concentrate on what seems to be going wrong, it is

because I still believe that what is wrong can be put right. In other words, I refuse to accept the sleep-walking fatalism of our time. When people say, as they are always saying: "Well, we can't do anything about it, can we?" I reply: "Yes, we can." Here I may be too optimistic, but nobody accuses me of that. And the most dangerous pessimist is the man who in the depths of his mind believes the facts to be so appalling that he refuses to accept them and pretends that somehow everything will be wonderful very soon. (It is his anger, when these facts are called to his attention, that makes him forget the ordinary courtesies and decencies of debate.) The basis of these essays is not imaginative insight, though it may achieve a phrase or two here and there, but just plain common sense. If we are in such a hurry to arrive somewhere, we had better ask ourselves now and again where we are going. It is no use heading for Coketown and telling ourselves we are going to the Lake District. We cannot cut down men's primary satisfactions and personal liberties and then tell them they are about to enjoy a fuller individual life. You cannot concentrate power and spread it at the same time. You cannot say you want men to appreciate the arts if you are doing everything possible to frustrate the artists. You cannot ask in the same breath for more fields and more motor highways and aerodromes, for fewer deaths on the road and for more, bigger, faster cars. You cannot expect schools to civilise children if the streets outside promptly turn them into barbarians. You cannot accept, even glorify, the lowest common denominator of taste and behaviour and imagine you are helping to create a new civilisation.

I have pointed out more than once that in our new society everything is becoming part of a huge idle show. Here are three recent examples, all the more important because they are taken from what are supposed to be dear to the heart of the people—loyalty to the Crown, sport, a decent regard for other people's feelings. When princesses were really princesses, huge headlines did not demand to know their intentions; when princesses are private persons, no such fuss will be necessary; but as it is, Princess Margaret has been treated as if she were a leading member of the cast of a gigantic public show.

Again, both in cricket and football, we have recently had spectators giving the players the slow handclap, to demonstrate that they were bored. But when men went to see Yorkshire defeat Surrey, or the Arsenal defy Wolverhampton, when in fact the spectators felt the match itself to be all-important, there was none of this slow handclapping. But now the games are part of the giant show, and if the show isn't good enough, give 'em the handclap.

Finally, the English people always used to have decent regard for other persons' feelings. But now they are to be amused on television by an elaborately contrived exhibition of other people under the stress of sudden emotion— a woman finds her house has gone, a man is brought face-to-face with an old sweetheart, and genuine bewilderment, grief, regret, deep embarrassment, are to be highlighted like juggling acts. We are almost within sight again of the Roman Circus, with minds if not bodies being torn to amuse the mob. Yes, I agree: so far the victims ask for it. But give the showmen time; and they might contrive a new twist or two.

All right—Jolly Jack's at it again. Where are the custard pies, boys? But while you are taking aim, children, just remember that most of you will have a great deal more of this world than he will. He is merely muttering a few words of caution on his way out.

ROUGH SKETCH
OF A LIFEBOAT

This piece is written for members of the English middle classes who are fond of the arts. I ask them first to believe, with me, that they are now living in a new society that cares little or nothing about their tastes and desires, that will leave them to fend for themselves. And the sooner we recognise these facts, the sooner we can begin to learn how to look after ourselves. We must do it. We have no 'They' to do it for us. It is useless waiting for the State, Big Business and Industry, the Trade Unions, to give us what we want. Nor have we enough votes, sufficient money, power in any form, to enforce our demands. From now on, as a group, we are out on our own. We must live as best we can.

What can we do by ourselves, with no help from the vast organisations? Once we have faced the facts of our situation, I believe we can do a good deal, and have a better time doing it than most of the pets of the new society will ever have. We can create instead of merely consuming. Moreover, we can create what we know we want, unlike the men of power, running mass communications, who are condemned to make what they think other people may want, people they mostly despise. If we can occasionally compel the big machines to serve our ends, so much the better; but we shall be well advised not only to consider what those ends are but also to have some plan of campaign. To that plan this piece is a modest contribution.

Publishing costs are rising. The young poet, short-story writer, essayist, will soon find it harder still to obtain a publisher. And what is fatal to the young writer is the feeling that he will never achieve print. (For this reason I have always held that if, for example, there is some money to be spent on poetry, it is more wisely spent on subsidies for poetry publication than it is when awarded to the poets themselves as fellowships, etc.) Perhaps more could be done with subscription than we ever try to do nowadays; though the English are poor subscribers, hating to commit themselves in advance to anything. It is on this rock that so many promising schemes for the arts strike, split, and founder. Our great-great-grandfathers were tremendous subscribers, but we have not such confidence. Still, it might be tried again, chiefly for mixed volumes of poetry and belles-lettres.

What is more likely to succeed, however, is a revival, preferably on a far larger scale, of the small semi-amateur presses and publishing enterprises of the type fairly common about thirty years ago. These would not only offer the young writer a chance of being published, they would also bring work they would enjoy to a lot of people at present wondering what to do with themselves. It may be objected that remote little presses would not be able to sell the books they published. But if there were enough of these presses, it would be possible to create a small wholesale company to distribute their publications, even to start a shop or two. I agree that experiments of this sort have rarely succeeded in the past. But people did not feel then that they were committed to a situation, as they ought to feel now. That is why it is so important that members of this group should realise how they are situated now, should plan for themselves as a society within a society.

It is a great pity that most writers on the Drama do not try to understand, and then make their readers understand, the economics of theatrical production. Nobody pays, or is willing to pay, three times the pre-war price for a theatre ticket, yet the costs, especially in the West End, have already more than doubled. A London production has to play almost to capacity to keep running at all. And costs will rise, even though actors are not immodest in their demands and playwrights take smaller royalties. Moreover, the Theatre, particularly in the provinces, is bound to suffer from the rapid development of TV. And the more initial capital a production requires, the less likely it is that that production will appeal to a minority audience. Already, experiment is almost impossible. People in their innocence are always asking me why I do not have my *Johnson Over Jordan* revived, not realising that such a production would be ruinous now, except to the Old Vic, which is solidly committed to Shakespeare.

What we need, if only to keep the players speaking directly to us, are new and comparatively inexpensive types of production, which have a chance of succeeding away from the mass audience. I offer two suggestions; other people may have better ideas. One is the 'platform play' like that piece Jacquetta Hawkes and I wrote, *Dragon's Mouth*, which was performed both in London and the provinces here some years ago, has been done abroad, and is to be produced in New York this season.

Pieces of this kind, which should be specially written rather than adapted from existing plays or novels, can be produced with the minimum of costume, properties, lighting effects, only ask for a few players and a platform, with some amplification of sound for larger halls. True, they are not plays proper, but more or less heightened debates, preferably within a dramatic framework; but on the other hand they give good players a fine chance of showing what they can do, they keep the dramatic spoken word alive, and actually increase the opportunities for elaborate and sustained speech. Young writers, producers, players, should give careful consideration to this new form.

Closer to the ordinary theatre, but avoiding a good many of its high costs, is "theatre-in-the-round", now being tried here and fairly well established in America and on the Continent. (Not long ago, the International Theatre Institute's quarterly, *World Theatre*, devoted an issue to it.) In this form the conventional picture-frame stage is replaced by an arena, almost like a circus ring. There are of course no sets, and just the barest minimum of furniture and props. Enthusiasts believe that it is better than our ordinary method of presentation, more imaginative, more intimate, more alive; but here I am recommending it simply in terms of costs. A theatre-in-the-round needs far less space than the usual playhouse; it can be built or adapted at a fraction of the cost, does not need its own building site, could be created out of a disused ballroom or the ground floor of a warehouse, and will comfortably seat several hundred people in a space that would be useless for an ordinary theatre. Again, the running costs are much smaller, for there are no sets to design, build, paint, put up and take down, and you can make do with only a tiny stage staff. Touring would be simpler and far less expensive. If a dozen large towns had theatres-in-the-round, it would be possible to send out tours costing so little that a minority audience could keep them going. And even though you may prefer the picture-frame stage, you must agree that intelligent plays in an arena are better than no intelligent plays at all.

As for music, where the immediate situation is not so desperate, I will only point out that here, in a fairly remote corner of the Isle of Wight, we are able to run successfully an annual Chamber Music Festival without asking for a penny of public money. For three nights we have some glorious music, including some of the best performances of certain works that I have ever heard anywhere, and everybody is happy. In fact, most of the music gains by being performed and heard away from the usual chilly little hall. and what we can do, miles from anywhere on this island, can easily be done elsewhere, in scores of places where most of the conditions are more favourable. There is also much satisfaction in helping to organise your own concerts, and I commend this music-in-the-country-house to everybody who cares about the art.

The visual arts, which cry out for the wealthy patron, cannot be brought easily into any scheme. I do not pretend to have the answers here. I can only offer a few scattered observations that might be helpful. First, about dealers. As a collector in a small way, I have done business with many dealers, most of whom I have liked. But they have one fault. They tend to keep the exhibiting, buying, and selling of pictures in a hushed, thick-carpeted atmosphere that belongs to another age. Duveen and his millionaires are dead. Many people, not rich but able now and again to find fifty or a hundred pounds for a picture, are afraid of venturing into London galleries, where, they imagine (and quite wrongly, as a rule), their fifty or hundred pounds would look like tuppence. And dealers should encourage and not discourage such potential patrons. They might also combine to send some of their pictures, perhaps long unsold, on a tour of the provinces, all marked with plain prices and no hush-hush genteel nonsense.

Pictures on loan, with a monthly renting fee, make no wide appeal—we seem to be possessive in our relation to the visual arts—but what, I think, has not been tried yet, and might have a much greater chance of success, is a properly organised system of exchange. This might encourage a number of people, who have neither much money nor much wall space, to buy pictures, knowing that they could exchange them from time to time, merely by paying a fee for the service of the agency. The fee would vary roughly according to the current value of the picture concerned. Thus, you bring in your picture, which is placed in Group D, and on paying the fee for this particular group you could take away any picture you fancied in that category. The scheme would be run at a loss at first, for the overheads would be considerable and the fees slow to arrive, but once it was going properly it would not only more than pay for itself but would sooner or later, I believe, greatly increase the number of patrons. And of course there is no reason why the exchange agency itself should not buy and sell works.

Anybody may have better ideas than these, and I hope some people will have. Let the ball roll. What I do claim is that here at least is an attempt to deal constructively with a situation that is bad and may soon, if we do nothing but grumble about it, get much worse. Let us begin by recognising, even at the risk of appearing to be too pessimistic, that nobody but ourselves will provide us with the sort of life we want. It is no use waiting for the power-mongers and the life-haters to do it. They have other plans, now maturing rapidly. We must create that life for ourselves. And if we have no longer the will, mind, and heart to create, and to enjoy creation, then we are already dying, and indeed would be better dead.

WHO
IS ANTI-AMERICAN?

Most of the reviews of *Journey Down a Rainbow* have been friendly—though there was the usual anonymous assassin in *The Times*—but too many of the reviewers have assumed that our book is yet another attack upon America. It is nothing of the kind, as we began the book by announcing. What I describe and denounce in my chapters is an economic-social-cultural system I call *Admass*. But *Admass* and the *Admassians* are not synonymous with America and the Americans, not even with Texas and the Texans, as again I was careful to point out. The sharpest and most urgent critics of *Admass* are themselves American. A large proportion of American writing is now devoted to questioning, challenging, satirising, and condemning the standards and values of *Admass*. This I know because I read a great deal of contemporary American writing: unlike many reviewers, who do not seem to be reading even the specimens of contemporary English writing sent to them by editors.

On the other hand, as I have indicated in our book and have suggested more than once in these columns, there is plenty of *Admass* now outside America. No doubt one finds the biggest, richest, gaudiest samples of the system across the Atlantic, but the rest of the world is hurrying to catch up. Post-war Britain is one of the most progressive

Admass colonies. That banquet the other week at the Guildhall, to mark the inauguration of commercial television, was pure *Admass* from soup to nuts. One reason why we are having such argument and fuss about Royalty is that it is caught between traditional Britain and the new *Admass* Britain, between the yearly portrait and the *Daily Sketch*. As I have said before, we English are more dangerously situated than the Americans because most of us, and reviewers to a man, do not realise we are in any danger. We think that if we can still toddle along to the Athenæum, the Beefsteak, and Garrick Clubs, the London Library, have our shirts made to measure, and hope to be made a Knight Commander of the Grand Order of Gentlemen of the Bedchamber, the *Admassian* jungle darkening the air all round us is no nearer than New York.

These reviews will add to my reputation, built up over a quarter of a century, as an anti-American. For one of the public rôles thrust upon me is that of *The Man Who Does Not Like America*. Except in private among a large circle of American friends, I have never been allowed to step out of this rôle. For twenty years, American reporters, after not being able to induce me to say anything rude about their country, have invented offensive remarks, all with a strong American accent, and have conjured them in and out of my mouth. I am the Gilbert Harding of Anglo-American relations. Dinner parties from Long Island to Santa Monica have been astonished when I have failed to insult everybody within hearing. Ordinary cheerful compliments have been probed for depths of savage irony. In descriptive essays of mine, filled with nothing but humorous exaggeration, there have been heard screams

149   L

of anger, thunders of rage. And nobody has ever bothered to inquire—and this is where real irony begins—why this hater and denouncer of America should be always going to the trouble and expense of finding his way back there.

At this point, the cynical know-all jumps in, to tell me that I am a shrewd fellow (which I am not) who knows how to collect dollars. And he is quite wrong, years out of date, for it is some time since the Americans paid handsomely to be insulted by visitors. An anti-American reputation is now a poor dollar-earner. The frequent visits only just pay for themselves. The truth is astonishingly simple: I go to America not only because I have professional business to attend to there but also because I like going to America. I criticise and grumble, of course, but that is largely because I have now an affection for the place and the people and am beginning to feel almost at home there. After all, I do still more criticising and grumbling here, where I am completely at home, in a country and among a people I love. You don't catch me grousing about Afghanistan and Patagonia, the Bolivians and Albanians: I don't know about them and don't care. But about America I do know and care.

To begin with, I have seen more of the country than most Americans have. I have a ripening acquaintance with its history and literature. I count myself as a friend of this nation, and so take with me the curiosity, the affectionate concern, and if necessary the frank criticism, of a friend. But I refer now not to America as it figures in cartoons, in articles by economic and foreign-affairs experts, in statistics or statements by mysterious official spokesmen, in any abstract account of human affairs. I know and have a growing affection for the real America, the place itself where the real people live: for Central Park on a Sunday morning, the magical towers of New York at dusk; for those white villages among the flaring woods of New England in the fall; for the majestic rivers I have crossed so many times, the trains hooting so mournfully as night descends on the immense sad plains; for the sparkle and sharp fragrance, the blue air and distant violet ranges of the desert; for the Pacific dimpling beyond the solemn groves of giant trees; and for all the people, or most of them, I have talked to, eaten and drunk with, cursed or kissed, across those three thousand miles. I can write and talk American. I could pass for one, at a pinch, if the cops were after me.

There is a further irony. There are people here who are never accused of being anti-American, who are praised over there for their friendship. And many of these are the very people who secretly loathe the place and detest its people, who would not care a rap if tomorrow the Atlantic and Pacific oceans met above Kansas City. They merely go whoring after American wealth and power. So long as they can use the Americans, they will contrive to put up with them. What they say in public, when they are wanting something America can give them, is very different from what they say in private, as these battered ears can testify. If wealth, power, influence, passed from the northern to the southern half of that continent, these fellows would be making the same smiling after-dinner speeches about the Argentine and Brazil—and the United States would be out. The test of friendship does not lie in idle compliments and lip-service but in a close continuing interest and an affectionate concern, which may at times necessitate plain speaking. The weakness of America's present position, which is roughly that of a newly arrived rich man at a decaying fashionable resort, is that this test cannot be easily applied, the whole scene being too strange and bewildering, with the result that Americans too often do not realise where their true friends are.

There is another difficulty. We all tend now—and Americans more than most—to imagine that the world of political intrigue, newspaper and radio comment, public relations and propaganda, cartoon adventures, is the real world. Given this false assumption, then if we do not like the State Department's handling of the German problem, we do not like America, would never want to see again those crimson maples, huge rivers, plains, deserts, sea-coasts both Atlantic and Pacific, would have done with all the hundred and fifty million persons who inhabit those regions. If we do not agree with Richard Nixon, any assorted Republican senators, the *Reader's Digest*, *Time*, the *Saturday Evening Post*, the Hearst Press, and Westbrook Pegler, then we cannot possibly want to enjoy another martini at the Coffee House Club, the Boston Symphony Orchestra, or the first sight of the desert from the Santa Fé *Chief*. It is as if when friends from New York arrived outside our door in the Albany, I did not invite them in until I had made sure they were in full agreement with our policy in Cyprus and were enthusiastic admirers of Eden, Butler, and Macmillan. Put like this, it seems altogether too idiotic, yet many 'anti-American' reputations, referred to over and over again in the Press, are based on no better foundation.

Take this journal itself. It has a notorious anti-American reputation; I must have seen a hundred references to it in the American Press. And what does this mean? No more than what I have already suggested, namely, that it has a reasoned dislike of certain American political attitudes and policies, themselves equally severely criticised by a host of Americans. What it does *not* mean—and what it would mean if it were properly used—is that this journal is written by men and women who detest the country, the people, the whole American idea, who wish the War of Independence had been lost or that Lee had finally defeated Grant, who sneer at American customs, habits, manners, accents, who go out of their way to avoid meeting Americans, who find nothing to admire in anything that comes from such a people, who in their heart of hearts regard America and the Americans as the enemy. This is to be genuinely anti-American. And in London, Paris, Rome and elsewhere I have met these haters of America (and some distinguished members of my profession were among them); but they were not on the staff of this journal; and I never remember seeing one of them described in the American Press as being anti-American. The bricks are always thrown in the wrong direction.

When Mrs. Smith tells Mr. Smith that his trousers are baggy and he needs a haircut, nobody accuses her of being anti-Smith. Now I have actually spent more time in America than I have in any country except England; more than I have in Scotland, Wales, Ireland. I have more friends in America than I have in any country except England. If I were to be kicked out of this country,

I should probably go to America, if it would have me. I have now an affection for it, and that is why I do not hesitate to criticise it. When I meet a friend I assume he would prefer my honest opinion to a vote of thanks. There is much in American life I do not like, just as there is much in English life that I do not like. But if I denounce *Admass* in *Journey Down a Rainbow*, that is not because it is largely American in origin and I long to have another crack at the Yanks. I do it because I believe the *Admass* system to be unworthy of the place, the people, and the astonishing revolutionary idea, unique in history, they represent. This is a nation that came out of a noble dream. If it is anti-American to remember that dream, which so many pro-Americans seem to forget, then I am indeed anti-American.

BOTTOMLEY

Mr. Julian Symons's biography of Horatio Bottomley is well worth reading. His cool precision is admirable; he is like a young research chemist examining a huge smelly three-ring circus. It is not his fault if I am disappointed. The fact is, I have been waiting over twenty years for somebody to produce a life of Bottomley; but I have always seen it as a big and rather Rabelaisian sort of book, not so much straightforward biography as satirical social history: *Horatio and his Times* or *The Bottomley Era*, crammed with quotations and amply illustrated.

Mr. Symons sent me back to a book that has been waiting on my shelves for many years: *The Real Horatio Bottomley* by Henry J. Houston, O.B.E. It was written while Bottomley was still alive but after he had been sent to prison. Houston was his chief organiser, secretary, valet and dogsbody. His book is cheap and nasty in appearance and even cheaper and nastier in its spirit, but it does offer the authentic glitter and flash of diamond cutting diamond. Houston was the thin canting rascal to Bottomley's fat impudent one; he was Ancient Pistol to Bottomley's Falstaff. Some of his anecdotes almost take us back to the Boar's Head and Eastcheap. For example, he tells us that Bottomley (who loved champagne and drank it all day long) grumbled excessively over a charge of two shillings for biscuits on a hotel bill while passing without remark an item of £6 12s. for wine. "Two shillings seems a devil of a lot for biscuits," cried Bottomley.

I never set eyes on Bottomley in his glory, but I remember seeing him shambling along Fleet Street and the Strand after he had come out of prison—old and broken, a fat man no longer fat and with his skin loose about him, his eyes dead, like a little old elephant. The face in his earlier photographs suggests a parody of some nobly public-spirited Victorian orator: broad and powerful, with the long upper lip and the wide mouth of the orator who is more than half actor; but the eyes are wrong and bad, being rather small, empty, and cold. He claimed to be Bradlaugh's natural son, but that old warhorse of the platform would have none of him: "Young Bottomley will turn out a bad man," he told George Jacob Holyoake. And certainly when we come close to him we find Bottomley an unattractive rogue, not only because he deliberately swindled his trusting public but even more because he was horribly selfish and cold-hearted in his treatment of the gang, all overworked and underpaid, that served him with such enthusiasm. On this close examination all that is left which does not repel is his astonishing impudence, often raised to such a height that it has in it something of the quality of great wit. But even this would not make him worthy of a large biography, ampler and livelier than Mr. Symons's. What makes me long for such a work is that just as Bottomley's face parodies that of some noble Victorian orator and Friend of the People, so his whole career is a kind of satirical parody of his age, and any detailed account of it would be devastating in its cynicism.

But who wants cynicism? About some things, I do, and would have it taught in schools. It is time some forms of solemn hocus-pocus were laughed off the stage of public life. We have been humbugged long enough. And this is where the life of Bottomley could be serviceable; perhaps there ought to be an edition for schools with plenty of notes. For he was the *ersatz*, poor man's, Great Public Figure, the tap room's Financier, Lawyer, Sportsman, Journalist, Politician. His impudent impersonations, finally landing him in jail, light up other men's character parts, glittering with honours and public esteem. For this perhaps he was punished. The final ruthless hounding down, then the determined cold-shouldering of the shambling old ex-convict, he probably brought on himself because he gave the game away. He was sent to jail and then to further oblivion not because he was too ambitious but because he was not ambitious enough, preferring some quick easy money to spend on bookies, women, and champagne, to the solid enduring prizes of Finance, Law, Journalism, Politics.

His financial career, which he began at a remarkably early age, was based on the simple and attractive idea, popular then and not entirely unknown even now, that it would be a good thing to acquire a lot of money without working for it. Unfortunately, his strategy was poor, his tactics crude, his campaigning careless. But suppose he had drunk barley water instead of champagne, spent more time in offices and board rooms and less on race courses, had seen more accountants and lawyers and fewer musical-comedy girls and willing waitresses, had made ten times as much money and had never been found out?

Have there never been, among the pillars of our society, men who were simply thinner, harder, wilier Bottomleys? They may not have broken the law as he did, may not have cheated as flagrantly. But I suspect they gave about the same value for money.

Again, the lawyers were bent on ruining Bottomley. It was his practice to conduct his own defence, which in his best days he did brilliantly. In his youth he attended the law courts as a shorthand writer, and though he may not have acquired much knowledge of the law itself, he learned a good deal about what happens at trials, all the shifts and devices of attack and defence, all the tricks of the trade. So for years, in one trial after another, this impudent amateur turned the tables on the professionals. He was a rogue, of course, whereas they were all scholarly men with a passion for justice, a hatred of prejudice and false reasoning, a contempt for publicity and fat fees. No wonder they disliked Bottomley so much.

The English people have always admired a Sportsman. Now Bottomley—to his credit, in my opinion—occasionally took his eighteen stones on to a tennis court and did not do too badly. But this does not make a Sportsman. On both the highest and lowest levels of English life it is agreed that the true Sportsman is the owner of racehorses. On Houston's evidence—and he is to be believed here—Bottomley had no real knowledge of horses, could not be trusted to buy a decent racehorse, and "even when he had a good horse he had not the vaguest idea of how to make the best use of it." But he knew what was required of a Sportsman. Even when he was fighting an election, he fought it partly as a Sportsman, and had his string of racehorses, wearing his colours, paraded through the constituency. I have a photograph of him before me in which he is displaying, a trifle gingerly, his favourite steeplechaser. He knew what belonged to a national figure; he could be a Sportsman too; with the same suggestion of highly satirical parody.

Then there was Bottomley the Journalist, a rôle he acquired early and played as long as he could hold the stage. His notion of journalism was simple and straightforward. He wasted no time discovering the truth or advocating unpopular causes. He accepted without question the favourite passions, prejudices, and idiocies of the mob, and then shouted his belief in them, his enthusiasm for them, at the top of his voice. What his readers and potential readers were against, he was ten times as much against. If they seemed to be changing their minds, he changed his a bit faster. Just before we got into the 1914 War, he wrote a red-hot article entitled *To Hell with Serbia*; but as soon as we were in, he wrote an equally fervent piece on *The Dawn of Britain's Greatest Glory*. He was the halfwit's loudspeaker. And both as proprietor and editor he never hesitated to distort any news or change the paper's views to suit his own prejudices, at times offering his services for sale. Here again, in all this, he is in character, offering us a vulgar burlesque of a typical important figure of our times. He grew up with the new journalism—in his youth he was actually associated with Alfred Harmsworth—and all he did later, in his own brash way, was to take the lid off it. The very papers that denounced him most savagely played the same game he had played, only rather more carefully and astutely.

159

His notion of journalism did not share his downfall.

Finally, there is the Politician. In politics his chief idea, perhaps his only idea, was that we should have a Business Man's Government: an idea we put into practice to some extent between the wars, with unhappy results. For the rest, he promised the electorate anything he thought it wanted, spent a lot of money in the local pubs and had himself shaved in all the barbers' shops of the constituency, arranged for his opponents to be heckled and for himself to be cheered at all meetings, and did everything to restore the grand old election atmosphere of Eatanswill. One of the few by-products of his political career was his vendetta against and final triumph over Charles Masterman, whom he drove out of politics, which were no better when robbed of Masterman's brilliant qualities. Bottomley's more successful fellow-politicians made use of him when they felt he had some power, and immediately dropped him when they knew he could be of no further use. True, he was never given any office—though for years he expected one—because he first entered the House with a dubious reputation; but during the First War and just afterwards, when English political life took a sharp turn for the worse and Bottomley himself commanded a vast mob of admirers, if his ambition had been harder and sharper, if he could have kept his hands out of the till and off the champagne and the girls, he might have become one of our Leaders and by now be the hero of one of those pompous and dropsical biographies, reviewed by Fellows of All Souls and read by nobody in their senses.

This existing biography, I noticed, was reviewed by two of our liveliest historians, who both assured us that nothing like Bottomley could happen again, that we have grown out of any childish confidence in such rogues. And with all due respect to two good minds—I say *Boo!* They are wrong, and dangerously wrong. Of course another Bottomley, with the same *persona*, the same repertoire, would not get anywhere now. But a new streamlined model of the artful and unscrupulous demagogue could easily outdistance Bottomley in a quarter of the time. We have now the perfect set-up for such a career. The new man would start as a TV personality, playing parlour games not too cleverly, not too foolishly, like the most charming young man at a party. He would be astonishingly and wonderfully ordinary, with not an eccentricity, not a sharp edge of personality, showing; none of your Hitler stuff, for we are not Germans wanting to be bullied. This chap would be more decently English than anybody outside the Hollywood English colony. And within three or four years he could capture almost any constituency. And after that he could leave fat old Bottomley panting miles in the rear. And no champagne, no musical-comedy girls; just an occasional Coke and an early bachelor bed every night; and in ten years he could be having some of us, if we lived that long, certified in batches. Bottomley? Bah!

THE UNICORN

We are losing because we are backing the wrong beast.
Our money should be on the Unicorn, not the Lion. We
forget that a Lion, a creature of this world, is subject to
time, that his claws are worn, his teeth mere stumps, his
eyes cloudy with age, that he has lost his speed and his
spring, that he has begun to shrink and is now dwarfed by
eagles that darken the sky and bears that come rearing out
of their winter caves as tall as fir trees. We have kept this
Lion in captivity too long. He has yawned and dozed
behind bars through too many years. When he roars now
it is only because his dinner is late, and no longer because
he wishes to challenge and terrify his enemies and ours.
All sorts of shabby beasts come trotting up, give his tail a
nip, screech in derision, and romp and prance within
sight of his sad yellow eyes. Now that he is so old, Lion-
taming is a corny act, well down on the bill. We know all
this, but habit persists: we still put our money on him, and
so lose it steadily.

Even now we are not risking the Unicorn, that odd
creature which found its way on to our coat of arms one
morning when all the sound types at the College of
Heralds were busy elsewhere. Some unsound fellow,
afterwards dismissed without a pension, opened a gate
not marked on any plan of the establishment, to admit
this fabulous monster. We tolerate him—after all, he

looks pretty on summer afternoons, and the ladies, bless
them, have always had a fancy for him—but, of course, no
solid money, direct from the City, backs his chance, even
at a sporting long odds. These are difficult times, when
a fellow has to be careful, so all the important money
must still go on poor old Lion. The careful, sound
chaps couldn't agree with one another more: it's lion
or nothing, let's face it. And so that same nothing, a
darkness in which now and again there glimmer phos-
phorescently some nightmare faces, creeps nearer and
nearer.

We prefer not to remember that the Unicorn, just
because he is not a creature of this world, escapes the
withering process of time. Unlike the Lion, he is as young
as ever he was, as swift and strong; his eyes are undimmed;
his single horn as tense and unyielding as it was many
centuries ago. He was magical then, he is magical now.
The enchanted kingdom he represents may be largely
forgotten, but it is still there, awaiting our discovery. But,
of course, if we lose faith in the Unicorn, if we are secretly
afraid of him, if we deliberately pretend he is not with us
now, then he cannot help us, for he is fixed, motionless and
powerless, until we speak the word that releases him.
Perhaps we leave that word unspoken, even declare we no
longer know what it is, because we think that any such
happy magic won't work. Too many of us islanders now
believe only in the other kind, a dark sorcery far removed
from the Unicorn and all he represents, and because we
believe in it we fasten its hold upon our minds.

Under the spell of this dark sorcery, probably designed
to make us follow the social insects, we prostrate ourselves

before the vast cement altar of the unimaginative, the uncreative, the unenterprising, the uninventive. It is the cult of a dreary conformity. Only the dullest is good enough for us. No man is fit to be trusted unless he is a bore. Anybody with an idea must be ignored, and soon may have to choose between exile and prison. Originality and insight and enthusiasm are a bar to advancement. A sound man—and we want no other kind—does not interrupt the march of the zombies. No risks must be taken; no crackpots encouraged; but under the guidance of thoughtful, responsible men, following a well-tried plan, we must move with care from one disaster to another. All gleams of hope may be extinguished, but in a decent, sensible manner. And mesmerised in the deepening gloom we hear the voices of authority in town halls, banqueting rooms, TV and radio, crying: "Mr. Chairman, friends, fellow somnambulists—Tonight I hope to be as repetitious, uninspiring, and as utterly devoid of creative ideas as I was when I last had the honour of addressing you . . ." And amid this mournful sorcery we forget that we still have the Unicorn.

Here we come to the grand ironic illusion. We islanders wish to impress the world. We might have decided to spend our time, trouble, money, putting ourselves into such a position that it did not matter whether the world was impressed by us or not (in which case it would have been vastly and astonishingly impressed by us); but the decision went the other way, so that we are committed to the task of impressing the world. *Hurray for the islanders!* the world must cry. But we do not hear these cries. Their absence is mentioned in the House, deplored in leading articles. The world now refuses to be impressed; it shrugs, jeers, sniggers, roars with laughter. Sounder and sounder men, absolutely dependable types, present at great expense our famous old Lion act, but everywhere it is a flop. "But look, please," they implore the audiences, "this is our Lion. *The* Lion. The one you read about at school —the identical Lion. Give him a little pat if you like, only, of course, be careful. Stop throwing orange peel, please. No, don't go away. See—he's opening his mouth. He may roar in a moment. Yawning? Never mind—hang on, chaps. In just a minute the Member for Podbury West, already making his mark in the House, will place his head in the Lion's mouth. Or—say the word, and the chairman of the Cosy Tin Motor Company—he'll be along in a jiffy—will ride on the Lion's back. No? I must say, you people are a bit much." It is all no use: the act is a flop.

But does nobody care about us islanders any more? Is there not even a murmur of admiration, a glance of respect? This is where the irony begins. Now I have done some travelling during the past eleven years, and all the way from Copenhagen to Cuernavaca, Tiflis to Tokio, the same thing happens almost everywhere. Fairly late in the evening, after a few rounds of bourbon-on-the-rocks, vodka, schnapps, saki, tequila, or whatever they are serving in those parts, the foreigners tell me that I am fortunate to be living in a country with such a noble creature, for which they have the deepest respect, the highest admiration. "Our Lion?" I exclaim, gratified but astonished. At once a barrage of emphatic negatives descends upon me. Who cares about that Lion? Please, is finish, that Lion. No, no, no, what is so wonderful about my island is its beautiful Unicorn. Boy, that's some beast! Comrade, we salute the British Unicorn! Honoured colleague, you must have for it much pride! And after another two rounds of whatever we are drinking too much of, they confess, most of them, that no such creature, so old and yet so young, so timeless, so potent in its magic, can be discovered now in their countries. And do we islanders realise how fortunate we are?

Unless the night is far gone, as a good Briton I pretend that always we are joyously aware of our good fortune. I suggest that the Prime Minister, the Chancellor of the Exchequer and all his senior officials, the Lord Privy Seal, the Leader of the Opposition, the Archbishops, assorted chairmen of federated industries, T.U.C., banks, coal and other boards, and anybody else of importance I can think of, are Unicorn attendants to a man. I describe how we cherish the lovely creature, taxing ourselves almost to bankruptcy to keep him glossy and proud. How can I reveal, at that time and place, the melancholy and ironic truth—that we are all so busy feeding and grooming and petting the mangy old Lion that we hardly notice the Unicorn? How can I confess my suspicion that some of my fellow islanders in authority, just intelligent enough to be aware of the Unicorn, only fear and hate him, and secretly hope that soon he will gallop away for ever? How can I explain that these men feel it would be safer to live where that fabulous single horn has reflected the moonlight for the last time? So although I may hear in my head these complacent or fearful voices, I say nothing about them to the foreigners, admiring me now as a visitor from the enchanted land of the Unicorn.

It is my belief—and nearly every bulletin I read or hear adds confirmation to it—that the Lion can do no more for us, that only the Unicorn can save us now. We have reached again, as we must do at irregular intervals, the hour of the Unicorn. I am seeing it, of course, as the heraldic sign and the symbol of the imaginative, creative, boldly inventive, original, and individual side of the national character. It is such qualities and what they have contributed to our national life and culture that are so genuinely and warmly admired by the rest of the world. It is the Britain of the poets and artists and scientific dis-coverers and passionate reformers and bold inventors and visionaries and madmen that still dazzles the world. If we want to impress it, this is what impresses it—the Britain of the Unicorn. If, as I believe, this country is in danger of decline, only the Unicorn qualities can rescue it. If we continue to suppress this side of ourselves, refusing to be imaginative, creative, inventive, experimental, we are lost. But now there is hardly an unsound Unicorn man to be discovered in our public affairs, hardly a single gleam of that legendary horn. Yet what else have we to offer the world that it wants from us? The Lion leaves it hostile or derisive. The old roar is wheezy, only displaying the worn teeth. Nothing there to awe distant peoples into submission, nor even to earn their respect. Commerce, then? Not without the Unicorn touch; not simply routine sound trading. Are we more industrious and painstaking than our competitors? (Don't make me laugh, chum.) What advantages now have our factories? Have we even many skills not easily acquired by disgruntled customers?

Do British salesmen outwit all others? What, in short, have we still got that our rivals haven't got?

To that final and terrible question I can only reply— *the Unicorn and all is represents*. Tricky, of course, risky, of course; mistakes will be made; all manner of rules and regulations may have to be broken; but a better prospect than that of millions on meagre rations, standing about again in hopeless streets, the victims of routine policies, timid conformity, minds without insight, courage and gaiety. So—up with the Unicorn! Make way for the unsound types, all those who made such a bad impression on the committee! Forward the imaginative men, the creators and originators, even the rebels and cranks and eccentrics, all those with corners not rubbed off, bees in their bonnets, fire in their bellies, poetry in their souls! It's nearly now or never. For if we don't back the Unicorn against the Lion, if we are not a boldly imaginative, creative, inventive people, a world that expected more of us will soon not even let us keep what we have now. The only future we can have worth living in is the one we greet, bravely and triumphantly, riding on a Unicorn.

THE STAGGERS
AND   NAGGERS

I am not sure I ought to be a guest at this celebration. Twenty-five years ago, I was not a friend of either bride or groom. I never contributed a line to the old *Nation*, and the closest I came to it was when, one afternoon in the early 'Twenties, I saw Mr. Leonard Woolf in the office and he suggested I should write a piece about what merchant sailors were reading. I replied truthfully—but, I believe, mildly—that the subject did not interest me. Mr. Woolf told a friend of mine, just after this encounter, that he thought I was going to knock him down. And years later, when we sat opposite each other at directors' meetings of this paper, I seemed to catch a speculative look in Mr. Woolf's eye. Perhaps he was deciding that I couldn't have knocked him down; and if so, he was right. The truth is, my face went on the stage in its teens, and has been playing in bad melodrama ever since. It knocks people down when the rest of me is wondering how to escape.

The closest I came to the *New Statesman* in the 'Twenties was when I visited Poland as a guest of the Government and Clifford Sharp, then editor, was with us, heading the huge fantastic binge. Over quadruple whiskies and vodka by the quart, Sharp set us right on all subjects, talking in crisp paragraphs, almost bringing out a new issue of his paper every forty minutes. After several interminable banquets, with toast lists that included everybody from George the Fifth to the assistant harbourmaster of Gdynia, Sharp vanished. I was told afterwards that he had been flown to some special clinic, examined for this, that, and the other, and then given all manner of treatments. And then, as suddenly as he had disappeared, he reappeared among us, pink of cheek clear of eye, alert of mind, ready to talk innumerable paragraphs and short leaders on all subjects. But for the Poles, who had so neatly restored him, he had nothing but a wave of dismissal. "Not an efficient people," he told us. "They'll never run a modern state properly." Such a judgment at such a moment, at once monstrous and insufferable, courageous and shrewd, was not untypical of Sharp and his paper, the *New States-man* of thirty years ago.

At that time and for some years later, Gerald Barry was my editor—an uncommonly good editor he was too—and my weekly pieces went into the *Saturday* and then the *Week-end Review*. I joined the *Saturday* contributors too late in the long career of that weekly to have any special affection for it; but the *Week-end Review* I loved throughout its brief bright day. I was essentially a *Week-end Review* man, and might almost be said to be still writing for it, occasionally helping it through that Great Turnstile. Experts of the weeklies, old review hands, tell me it was never a really solid job, never taken seriously in the House and the political clubs: it was not sufficiently well-informed. But what it lacked in these departments it more than made up for in other parts of the paper, where Gerald Gould, Ivor Brown, Earle Welby, L. P. Hartley, and the rest of us had our say. The specialities of the house were good writing, wit, and zest. Every number was the gay Last Stand of the brilliant broadbrow, himself a doomed type. But its spirit was never entirely quenched. It haunts one part of High Holborn like a will o' the wisp. It could make no marriage, this *wunderkind*, but it was adopted by the happy pair whose nuptials I ought now to be celebrating.

In the 'Thirties many of us felt that the *N.S. & N.* was like a pantomime horse played by two men who had quarrelled. This difference between the Socialist front half and the æsthetic back half has often been noticed; but I happened to suffer from it more than most. Nearly everything I wrote was praised on the fourth page only to be denounced on the twentieth. On one floor of the editorial office I was nearly a hero, and on the other I was a vulgar fraud. Against the adverse criticism of the boys upstairs I sent letter after letter of passionate remonstrance, only to be told by the editor that all this abuse was really an indirect tribute to my size, importance, grandeur, a proof that I was a man well worth denouncing and insulting. Shortly after I became a director of the paper, I was foolish enough to write something faintly derogatory about a series W. J. Turner (that fine poet) was editing. At once the enraged Walter Turner slammed in a letter telling the world that for years I had been notorious for my conceit, arrogance, refusal to take any criticism—a V_2 of a letter. "Abominable, I agree," said the editor, "and of course we wouldn't have published it if you hadn't been a director."

Let us consider this editor before saluting the paper

itself. I find three layers in him. There is first the brisk superficial optimism that surprises people who meet him for the first time. Below that is of course an inky depth of pessimism in which lurk Disaster and Total Ruin, waiting to emerge at the hour of doom. But deeper still, among subterranean fires, is a core of unconsidered and unrealised optimism, where the essential self of our editor is having a hell of a good time. I have known this man off and on for more than five-and-thirty years, since I first saw him, a young Cassius, in the hall at Magdalene sitting at the feet of Graham Wallas; and I repeat that his essential self has a hell of a good time. He enjoys living here and now as few of us do. Let him protest as much as he pleases, this is his age: he might have bespoke it. I remember his arriving some years ago for a week-end at my house in the country, loping in, ready for anything from table tennis to toccatas, with fire in his cavernous glances; and he announced almost at once, as if bringing a great treat for the whole family, that we were probably within twelve hours of total, final, utterly ruinous war. Millions of men would be on the move, the air would be darkened by bombing planes, he declared, making a damned good lunch. By the time he was ready for coffee and a cheroot, western Europe was a smouldering ruin. Can you wonder that at the time when we were losing everywhere from North Africa to Singapore, his paper's circulation was taking the most prodigious leaps in the history of our weekly journalism? It had zest and guts.

A maddening, intolerable, insufferable paper! Of course. We often hear people say they would not have certain things given them. And how rarely they mean it!

But the man I heard at the club meant it when he said he had begged for no more issues of this paper to be sent to him, because he hated to think that it was in the house. I understood him; I sympathised with him. But I knew too that he had decided to start the retreat from life, to take himself out of sight and sound of the dusty, glaring arena. His favourite periodicals from then on would be nothing but programmes for memorial services. He had given up the fight for the good life. Of course I believe that hardly anybody who writes regularly in these columns understands what the good life is. Whereas in the 'Thirties I disagreed with one half of the paper, now I disagree with both halves. When I have the energy to fight my way in here, I do it to denounce everything the paper is commonly supposed to stand for. But after all, it stands for me too. I have had more quarrels with this paper than with any other, and I would rather write for it, rather read it, than I would any other. It is maddening because it reminds you of things you don't want to be reminded of. It is intolerable because it chooses topics long before they are respectable and cleaned-up for the leader writers. It is insufferable because it keeps nagging away like a decent man's conscience. It is in fact not unlike the opposite partner in a sensible, lasting marriage. Which brings me—and very neatly too, if you want my opinion—to the silver wedding we are celebrating.

THE OUTSIDER

Two clever young men, newcomers on the scene, have
done very well this summer out of what one of them calls
The Outsider. This newcomer is, of course, Mr. Colin
Wilson, whose dashing study of *The Outsider* has had such a
well-deserved success. The other is Mr. John Osborne,
whose first play, *Look Back in Anger*, itself a full-length
portrait of a *lumpen* Outsider, pulled so many persons of
distinction into the Royal Court Theatre, after having had
some dismal notices from the daily Press, like many
another first play trying to say something. The gossip
writers have told us that both these clever young men have
been on the telephone all day and half the night refusing,
accepting, or agreeing to consider wonderful offers from
publishers, editors, play and film producers. And if this is
true, then I for one am delighted, all the more so because
after thirty-five years as a professional writer, years during
which many of my friends and I have done pretty well in
various departments, I have never succeeded in penetrat-
ing into, never have had any first-hand experience of, this
world the gossip writers know in which the telephone fairly
blazes with dazzling offers.

So it looks as if these young Outsiders are after one
bound further *In* than most of us have ever been, living as
we do in some modest suburb of the spirit, neither quite
Out nor In. Now they will have to be very careful, dined

and wined as they will be by some of our most artful
Insiders. For example, Mr. Osborne has in him a streak of
Barriesque gooey sentimentality, which already can see
husbands as bears and wives as teeny-weeny squirrels, that
he will have to restrain when the Insider boys go after it.
Edwardian though I may be, I should like to see him
harder, not softer. I say Edwardian, because his chief
character, the *lumpen* Outsider, is caught reading one of
my pieces in this paper, and dismisses it and me as so much
Edwardian nostalgia. A bit much, as people like to complain, seeing that most of my contributions to this paper
have been attempts to take a genuine look at our present
time—discovering, for example, political apathy about
two years before the politicians and leader-writers found it
out.

There are some strange goings-on in this play—for
childless young women rarely start ironing about six
o'clock on Sunday evening, and by that time most young
men with a passion for the Sunday papers have read them
hours before—and too many essential points are not made
and other points made too often; but it held my attention
(even if I did not roar my approval as often as the *lumpen-
intelligentsia* that night in the audience seemed to do) just
because it is a reasonably honest portrait of a young man
of our time. This young man was rotten with self-pity—
his girls were worth ten of him—but that does not make
him less representative of this age. (Many successful
American novels, like the reviewers who praise them, are
also loaded with self-pity.) His tragedy is that, while he
has enough zest and energy to keep his loud complaining
talk going night and day, he has not sufficient to make

more of his own life and to help other people to make more of theirs. As he sees himself, he is a revolutionary without a cause. He arrived just after the revolution that never happened. Our politicians can do nothing with him, because they cannot inspire him—and he needs to be inspired—and they cannot successfully nag him, if only because he never stops nagging himself. He ought to emigrate to a country where he can either man the barricades or make some quick easy money and spend it riotously. Low-level security, perfect for people who are anxious not to die rather than to live, is not what this type needs. He is, in his own way, one of Mr. Colin Wilson's Outsiders.

Mr. Wilson's book, as so many people have already pointed out, is a remarkable production for a young man of twenty-four, although, as nobody seems to have pointed out, it is also the kind of book you want to write when you are twenty-four and, if you develop (as Mr. Wilson shows every promise of doing), when you are forty-four wish you had not written. Part of its success—and this takes nothing away from Mr. Wilson's achievement—is due to the fact that our more mature critics ought to be writing books with this breadth and attack, and are either too timid or too lazy to do it. So Mr. Wilson, piling up his notes in reading rooms and then desperately tearing into the big job, well deserves to succeed. He is all over the place, bringing in every name he can remember, but it is fun lumbering after him. There is some rough going on the way. He seems to me to lump together, simply as Out-siders, too many people who are sharply and often pro-foundly different. And the dichotomy of Outsider and

Bourgeois is altogether too simple. Like most clever young men, hurrying home with a pile of books and glowering at the passers-by, he magnifies the gulf between men of genius and ordinary stupid people, and is too certain all the latter are what they appear to be at a first impatient glance. He cannot believe that stockbrokers may have strange dreams, that butchers cutting off chops may be touched with intimations of immortality, that the grocer, even as he hesitates over the sugar, may yet see the world in a grain of sand.

This bring us to Blake, who is included among Mr. Wilson's Outsiders. But a category into which can be shovelled Blake and Sartre, van Gogh and Bernard Shaw, George Fox and Nijinsky, is becoming altogether too broad. Mr. Wilson even accepts the last published work of H. G. Wells, *Mind at the End of its Tether*, as proof that Wells, just before he died, changed from Insider to Outsider. But Wells was always less of an Insider than Mr. Wilson imagines—he could be described as an Outsider at heart always vainly and impatiently trying to find an Insider's cure and solution—and that strange psychological document, *Mind at the End of its Tether*, seems to me a projection on to the universe of his own dissolution already accepted by his unconscious. Again, while it may be true that all Outsiders cannot complacently accept this world and this life, feel that all is strange and unreal, and must tell the truth at all costs, their personalities are so widely various, they represent so many different psychological types, that any discussion of them based on their common likeness does not take us very far. And clearly a man might be an Outsider and not be a

genius nor yet have any recognisible talent, but just be an
endlessly tiresome talker, like the young man in Mr.
Osborne's play. There are more of these Outsiders than
there are of men with genius or talent, but Mr. Wilson
keeps clear of them in his book, just as the rest of us try to
avoid them in life.

Even Outsiders with genius or great talent are often
seen to be lop-sided, too introverted, unhappily egoistical.
If they are artists—and serious contemporary art, in
almost all forms, is now often held to be the product of this
temperament and of no other—their work may have a
strange fascinating intensity, almost a hypnotic power,
and yet leave us feeling dissatisfied and uneasy. Nor does
this mean that it is disturbing our bourgeois complacency,
for we may not have any to disturb. (The really complacent bourgeois do not bother about serious contemporary art.) We may feel dissatisfied and uneasy because
this art is not giving us what we want from art. Sometimes it is as if we went hungry into a restaurant and were
served with broken glass. I remember a few years ago,
when somebody close to me was desperately ill, wandering
round the West End one afternoon, just for a brief break,
and coming upon a shop that had just been opened, to
offer us all that was most significant and searching in the
art and letters of our time. I knew there would be no
soothing syrup in that shop, did not expect it, but did think
there might be something that would give a lift to the
spirit. But no such luck. The massed Outsiders glared at
me out of ruin and horror.

But who, Mr. Wilson will ask, are responsible for this
ruin and horror? The Insiders, he will triumphantly reply.

But if the Outsiders have all the genius and great talent, could they not occasionally cast about for something that might possibly inspire Insiders with a little courage, faith, hope? Insiders change too, and now are hardly the complacent bourgeois of Mr. Wilson's text. After all, this is 1956, not 1856; people are reading Bertrand Russell and Arnold Toynbee, not Macaulay. I write as one not entirely committed by temperament to either party, being an Inside Outsider or an Outside Insider, for I have it on the highest authority that I am balanced between extreme introversion and extraversion. But while I have a natural sympathy with most rebels, while I understand more or less what the serious Outsider artist is up to, I can never help feeling uneasy and vaguely depressed when I run into the whole procession of Twentieth Century arts, for example in such a book as William Gaunt's *The March of The Moderns*. What a weird gang it is! What a hell broth and Bedlam of appalling handicaps—like a doctor's museum and a psychiatrist's casebook—that have to find compensation through this wealth of talent! And how far gone our society must be if all its most representative art must be fetched from the misfits! Where now are all the glorious old Insider Artists, who were the ordinary men of their time writ large, who created out of an abundance of energy and joy, who praised God for all their fellows? We are trapped now, it seems, in a most vicious circle, for we work to produce ruin and horror, our artists are those on the Outside who have a blazing vision of this ruin and horror, we turn from life to the arts to encounter more ruin and horror, and in our despair, finding neither the courage and hope to do better nor even the will to endure, we pile up the ruin, heighten and deepen the horror. Mr. Wilson declares—and I agree with him—that the Outsider demands a religious solution. But if the Outsider is poisoned by an embittered egoism, if he wants to hurt and not to heal, if there is more hate than love in him, if he uses his gifts to deny the essential goodness in life, always adds ruin to our ruin, horror to our horror, can he bring us nearer to that solution? We are waiting for God, not for Godot.

SHAW

Nearly forty-five years ago, when I began writing a weekly page for the *Bradford Pioneer*, I became acquainted with a group of enthusiastic Shavians, who lived for the Master's next work or pronouncement. When they attended one of his plays, everything in it—costumes, wigs, and all— brought screams of laughter from them. They seemed to me then rather silly people, and I doubt if I would change my mind now. They also gave me a prejudice against their wonderful, inimitable G.B.S. and it took me years to get it out of my system, if ever I completely did. I met him on a good many occasions, not only on committees and at parties but also under his own roof and mine; but though we had the theatre as common ground, I never felt at ease with him: he was too much my senior, nearly forty years; he might be considerate both as host and guest, as indeed he was, but it was clear that I was heavily addicted to all the smaller vices from which he was free; on the other hand, he seemed to me the victim of two vices from which I felt myself to be reasonably free, namely, talking too much and showing off. But of course by this time he was fixed in his rôle of The Ancient of Days; I never even caught a glimpse of him—though I might easily have done, for he often visited Bradford—in his earlier and greater rôle as a red-bearded, Jaeger-type Mephistopheles.

It was the greater rôle because, to my mind, that was

when his best work was done. Although he became almost a symbolic figure of old age, it was G.B.S. in early middle-age who wrote the plays that will last longest. I am not even excepting *Saint Joan* and *Heartbreak House*. For a time I thought the latter his supreme masterpiece, but on the last occasion when I took in that third act, when we were all sitting under a giant bomb, its emotional impact seemed inadequate. This inadequacy has to be faced in Shaw. When I was a boy, ordinary stupid people thought him a self-advertising intellectual clown, who would say anything to attract attention. This view of him was dismissed with contempt even by those, like Chesterton, who sharply disagreed with him. And, of course, it was nonsense. Yet there was in it, as there often is in the judgments of ordinary stupid people, a valuable grain of truth. He held many beliefs but he did not hold them as most of us do. He never appeared to be emotionally committed to them. He could advance or defend them without anger. His warmest admirers tell us that this was because he was almost a saint. The opposite party say it was because he had a great deal of the charlatan in him. What is certain is that his peculiar relation to his beliefs gave him both the strength and the weakness characteristic of him.

He and Wells, whom I knew better than I did Shaw, offered some valuable contrasts. Wells always behaved far worse than Shaw; he was too impatient; he made mischief; he lost his temper and screamed insults and slander (Belloc once said that Wells was a cad who didn't pretend to be anything but a cad; that Bennett was a cad pretending to be a gentleman; that Shaw was a gentleman pretending to be a cad.) These tantrums threw into relief

Shaw's patience and good humour and courtesy; and in any debate between these two, G.B.S. would win easily on points. Yet for my part I was always admiringly and affectionately aware of H. G.'s honesty of mind, his frankness, his raging desire to discover and to announce the truth. To those redeeming qualities it seemed to me that Shaw opposed something personally attractive and polemically formidable, but disingenuous and dubious.

Thus, Shaw might win the argument about Stalin and the Soviet Union, but it was Wells who was nearer the truth, and was not playing any monkey tricks with his own values. Sometimes, both when I read him or heard him in private, I felt that Shaw deliberately switched off his imagination when dealing with certain topics. It is not that he was downright dishonest, but that he refused to follow his debating points into the world of flesh and blood. So he could defend or even admire dictators when he must have known that he could never have endured their authority. He could cheerfully advocate the 'liquidation' of anti-social types, as if they were merely being barred from a summer school. He did not see them as real people, shrieking and bleeding, but as creatures of paper and ink, characters with no entrances in the third act.

I never felt he came through into the world that followed 1914. Often he seemed to have persuaded himself that we were all still in the Edwardian world of debate, where the man who disagreed with you so violently on the public platform would be found, smiling a welcome, at the next week-end house-party. During that long fine afternoon it was fun to listen to a witty Irish Socialist, even if you did not believe a word he said. Later, especially after 1917, it was different. There had arrived the world of passports and visas, secret police and strange disappearances, labour camps and gas chambers. Even in England there were changes. The Socialist was no longer a crank but a menace; it was fortunate for G.B.S. that he now became a grand old man, and escaped most of the new hard abuse and the elaborate smearing.

Again, there is to my mind something dubious, disingenuous, too, reminiscent of those rather fatuous Shavian groups, in much of his handling of our non-intellectual, emotional life. He would pretend to be through with sex, as if it were fretwork or stamp-collecting, when really he had hurriedly by-passed it. This pretence almost ruins some of his plays. Those maternal managing heroines of his ought to have had fourth acts composed for them by Strindberg. As for his assorted kittens, from Cleopatra to Orinthia, they are hygienic toys with never a gland in working order between them. No wonder that his greatest part for an actress is Joan of Arc.

All this seems very damaging, and so it would be if it were not for the fact that most of his plays rest on his strength as well as on his weakness. Because he could hold his beliefs in his own peculiar fashion, keeping them free of negative emotions, he was able to create his own kind of comedy, good enough to put him among the world's great dramatists. This comedy of his has light without heat. The superbly theatrical wit crackles and dazzles and strikes without wounding. Behind the cut-and-thrust of the talk, like some smiling landscape behind a battle scene, is a vast golden good humour. The master quite early of a

magnificent debating style, he heightened it and orche-
strated it to provide us with this comedy of argument, the
Mozartian opera of witty debate. And this is not far-
fetched, for it was opera and not other men's plays, the
stuff he had denounced as a critic, that offered him
models. He told me himself how he nearly always began
without any ground-plan of action, hearing and not seeing
his characters, trying a duet, then a trio, then perhaps a
full ensemble. It is this method, together with an absence
of fine shades and atmosphere, that explains why reper-
tory companies in a hurry so often choose a Shaw play.
You have only to learn the lines, slam them across, and the
piece comes to life.

Treat Chekhov in this hell-for-leather style and you
have nothing that the Russian master had in mind. For
these two, the best who have written in this century, are
complete opposites. And here is an odd thing. It is the
dramatically simple, forthright Shaw and not the delicate,
evasive Chekhov who is the dangerous influence. No
playwright was ever the worse for being influenced by
Chekhov. But Shaw's direct influence has been the kiss of
death: no survivor is in sight. This is not hard to explain.
Chekhov opened out a new dramatic method, whereas the
Shaw play is a highly personal *tour de force*, demanding his
unique style and temperament. I never felt myself that
G.B.S. was really interested in dramatic method, though,
of course, he may have tired of the theatre by the time I
knew him. He despised the content of the plays he
criticised in the *Saturday Review*, but he was not above
using some of their oldest tricks. When an act was getting
a bit dull he would bring on a gorgeous uniform or some

fancy dress; and some of his deliberate clowning, as distinct
from the expression of his wit, is just embarrassing.

Saint or charlatan, he was Irish, not English. What
would have been fighting words in a Cockney or Lancashire accent seemed delicious banter in that rich, soft
brogue. His debating tricks, which were often outrageous,
were in the Dublin tradition, and so, of course, was his
assumption of a public character part, starring in a cast
that had Wilde, George Moore, Yeats, 'A.E.', James
Stephens, all playing character parts. Like Chekhov's
Gaev, he was "a man of the 'Eighties"—with some Edwardian ripening. After that, he was with us but not of us.
Like a man in a cautionary fairy tale, he had his wish
granted—to live a long time—and it was all different and
wrong. He became—and who can blame him?—a very
vain old super-V.I.P. I remember once coming across
him at the Grand Canyon, and found him peevish, refusing to admire it, or even look at it properly. He was
jealous of it. Later still, the crisply assertive style, which
he kept almost to the very end, deceived people into
imagining that he was still thinking hard when he was
often being rather foolish. His wife was no intellectual
giant, but it seemed to me that her mind was still open long
after his had finally closed.

You might say that he made up his mind too early,
which gave him an immense advantage in debate, arming
him at all points, but cost him something in wisdom.
Bertrand Russell, who had known him a long time, said
that G.B.S. was an immensely clever man but not a wise
man. He seemed to me to have a sort of natural wisdom
in his ordinary dealings with life (he must have given

people in private more really good advice than any other man of his time), but to be perverse, obstinate, cranky, wrong-headed, in his positive philosophy. He was, in fact —and came at just the right moment—a great destroyer, head of the Victorian rubbish disposal squad. He hid any doubts he might have about his positive wisdom in quick mocking laughter, just as he hid so much of his face behind a beard, red and white at the proper seasons. But because he was an iconoclast, this does not mean, as many people imagine, that all his work will 'date' itself into obscurity. I suspect that all the 'dating' that can happen has already happened. His best pieces, those comedies unique in style and spirit, have the vitality that defies time and all social changes. Their character, their appeal, may be different —for notice how early plays like *Arms and the Man* and *You Never Can Tell*, once thought to be grimly shocking, now seem to bubble and sparkle with wit and delicious nonsense—but they will be alive. And existing still behind the work will be the memory and the legend of the man, half saint and half clown, preposterous in his Jaeger outfit and assorted fads, glorious in his long stride towards some kingdom worthy of the spirit—the wittiest of all pilgrims, humming an air by Mozart.

THE POPULAR PRESS

The chief complaint against the popular Press is that it panders to the lowest tastes of the mob. It is morbidly sensational, we are told. It is determinedly and elaborately obscene. It asks us to buy it so that we can read about what happens to girl drug-addicts, what the Italian parlourman did in the bathroom, why the two blonde schoolgirls vanished from home, what orgies took place in the villa. Colossal circulations, the largest in the world, are built up in this fashion. Freedom or no freedom, indignant moralists tell us, we must put a stop to it.

This crusade cannot find a recruit in me. For years I have regularly bought a Sunday newspaper (though it is not the only one I buy) that has specialised as long as I can remember in reporting, with as much detail as it is allowed to print, all the police court cases that involve our fancier sexual antics. Probably I have a dirty mind. Certainly I have a mind sharp-edged with curiosity, and it is in these shocking columns, crammed with solemn police evidence, that I discover how many odd people live in this odd island of ours. It is here the lid comes off, to reveal characters and situations so wildly improbable that no novelist or dramatist with a reputation for realism would ever dare to make use of them. I remember, among many treasures, a scene between two horrible schoolgirls and a terrified gravedigger that even Webster or Tourneur would have reluctantly rejected.

It is a mistake to suppose that there is here anything new. I remember dining, many years ago, with the portentously respectable peer who at that time owned this particular Sunday paper. He told me—and I believed him, and still do—that, contrary to general opinion, the Victorian Sunday papers were ten times worse than his. For example, the fascinating Dilke case was reported with a wealth of obscene detail that would not be tolerated now. Our great-grandparents were even more excitedly curious about 'orgies' than we are. What a word of power that is—*orgy!* I once thought of writing a story about a retired man of means who went round the world looking for an orgy, only to be told everywhere that he had arrived just too late ("You ought to have been here before they cleaned this place up, old boy," he would be told at the Bougainvillea Club), but perhaps returning home, old and weary, to find the police raiding an orgy there.

Though I do not seriously defend all this salacious stuff, it seems to me comparatively harmless when it is compared with the attention given to sadistic murder and all the pathological muck it dredges up. To my mind one of the strongest arguments against capital punishment is that the shadow of the hangman and the gallows brings a kind of awful dignity, fascinating to shallow minds and trivial lives, to characters and events that ought to be filed away in the records of police inspectors and psychiatrists. Once the judge has put on his black cap, a host of foolish people, denied a conscious entrance into our ancient myths, are stirred somewhere in the depths of their unconscious, and see in any shabby little psychological misfit, doomed to be destroyed, the magical gleams of a Baldur or a Lucifer. And the popular Press, which often shows an instinctive feeling for the shadow shows of the unconscious, thunders out like Wagnerian brass these *leit-motifs* of doom, adding to the vague old magic the new enchantment of *publicity*. For we live in an age when publicity does not mean merely writing large what was written small before, so that what was originally silly is only sillier when immensely enlarged. No, in our day, publicity, in all but the most horrifying matters, turns into an added quality, bestowing distinction, a face that can be recognised among the millions of masks.

This brings us to what is really wrong with the popular Press of this country, to a fault in which it leads the world, to the point where it undoubtedly is beginning to corrupt its readers. What is wrong with the British popular Press is neither its obscenity nor its sensationalism, both of which may be found in larger measures in newspapers elsewhere: it is its determined and ever-increasing *triviality*. Let me add at once here that I am not alone in believing this. It is the view of a great many intelligent journalists, who may shrink from stating it in public but are almost luridly forthright about it in private—as I discovered, among other places, in a Press club overseas, not long ago. There I heard newspapermen belonging to several nations declaring that our post-war journalism was unmatched in its insistence upon the trivial.

A little later, to make some comparison for myself, I bought several issues of New York's notorious 'tabloids' and went through them carefully. True, there was all manner of rubbish in them; their general tone and taste were awful. But there was a great deal more news and sensible comment in them than can be found in our worst sheets. An intelligent man could spend more time reading them. They offered far more glimpses of the real world. They might be running various stunt features of their own, but they were not running them to the exclusion of all manner of important news and views. They were still newspapers, not throwaways for a three-ring circus. When the nonsense was drained off, there remained a good five-cents-worth of reading matter. They did not make you feel that their managing editors must have been recruited from the sillier types of shopgirls and chambermaids; a few adult males had had some part in the enterprise. Yet I well remember the time, when I first went to New York, when I stared at these same newspapers in disgust, hoping that ours would never be as bad. Some of them now are much worse.

It will be said that a successful popular newspaper reflects the interests and tastes of its readers, and would not be successful if it didn't. If our papers are trivial, it is because our people are trivial. If Miss Marilyn Monroe's marriage or Lady Docker's wardrobe is given more space and attention than anything else, then that is because the bulk of readers are more passionately concerned and curious about Miss Monroe or Lady Docker. If 'TV personalities' get more space than all our artists, scientists, philosophers, scholars, put together, that is because the millions who read the popular Press are also the millions who watch television. So runs the argument, and it is not easy to rebut. Nevertheless, it is too simple. We have passed the point at which our mass media are mere reflections of the mass mind. Now they can create the taste by which they are judged. Thursday's paper is eagerly read because it offers further news of what was made important by Monday's and Tuesday's papers. Miss Monroe and Lady Docker may be the people's darlings, but they were Fleet Street's first.

An experiment ought to be tried. Let six editors, perhaps with some backing from the B.B.C. and I.T.A., agree to turn the big spotlight for a week or so on a kitten called Snookums. Every day there is a lead story about Snookums. Large photographs decorate the front page. Everybody connected with Snookums, including the milkman who delivers its milk, is interviewed and photographed. There is no escaping Snookums. And before the end of the second week I suspect you could draw a large crowd anywhere by announcing that a glimpse could be caught of Snookums. Millions of people would believe that Snookums meant something important in their lives. And editors not in the original conspiracy would hastily climb on to the Snookums band-wagon and, if asked why they filled their columns with such stuff, would indignantly retort that it was their business to give their readers what they wanted. Yet nobody would have wanted Snookums.

We are rapidly arriving at a time—if, indeed, we have not already arrived at it—when masses of people do not really want anything until they are told they want it. A thing becomes important because they read about it in the Press or hear about it on TV and radio. More and more of their interests and tastes have to be created rather than reflected or catered for. This does not mean that if the

Daily Flash and the *Sunday Bash* linked up with the Third Programme, cricket and football grounds and cinemas would be deserted, so that Kafka and Monteverdi could be uproariously enjoyed elsewhere. It is not quite as simple as that. But it does mean that more and more a vast public decides what is and what is not important on the basis of the attention it receives in the Press. Only so much attention, so much space and time, can be given. If Snookums has to be highlighted, then all the work of the U.N. special agencies may have to be left out. If television announcers and models are in, then teachers and nurses are probably out. So day after day a false picture of the world is flashed on to millions of innocent minds, whose education, no matter how much we spend on it, largely fails to screen them.

Is this emphasis upon triviality deliberately aimed at by proprietors and editors? In a few instances—yes. There are some men in this trade who hate their customers, and delight in cramming them with muck. The rest go round and round in a fairly vicious circle of professional cynicism and commercial cunning. (Happy men may exist on the upper levels of this industry, but I have yet to meet one of them.) What all but the most intelligent and the most depraved, who don't care a damn, choose to forget is that the morons they are helping to produce are in fact the inhabitants of this country, the people upon whose future efforts and intelligent co-operation we shall depend for our existence. And I for one do not give a trivial Britain a very long, prosperous life. The world will not help to maintain us in our second childhood.

TELEVIEWING

Down here on the island, where I have rented a fine large set and where we have a powerful transmitting mast not far away, I am a Viewer. We keep the set in a room originally intended for music, and I can sit in the dark there, viewing and viewing, without disturbing the rest of the household. I lie back in an armchair, put my feet up on a stool, and smoke and view away. Except when there are Test Matches, I do all my viewing after dinner. Wheezing a bit, heavy with food and drink, I waddle along the hall, switch on the set, drop into my chair and put my feet up, then peer into my magic mirror like a fourteen-stone cigar-smoking Lady of Shalott. At first I told myself that I watched the set and its antics for strictly professional and technical reasons, but lately I have not had even a shadow of that excuse. I am simply one of the Viewers. I have already passed uncounted hours half-hypnotised by the jiggling and noisy images. Sometimes I wonder if I am going out of my mind. We have been told that the worst is over after about four years, but long before that my outlook will have been so completely changed that I shall be a different person. I shall probably be removed to an old man's home. Let us hope these places are equipped with good TV sets.

In my capacity as a Viewer, I have no intention of criticising adversely and in detail the way things are done.

Given this strange medium and their own particular responsibilities, the people directing and handling the medium do almost all that can be reasonably expected of them. Most of them, I know, are enthusiasts; if removed from TV they would feel they were in exile. I don't imagine I could do it better myself. I think I would be far worse than they are. Most of the familiar jeers and sneers at their efforts seem to me quite unfair. The difficulties they have to face are too lightly disregarded. The critics who attack them make little or no allowance for the black magic of the medium itself, always discussing the entertainment provided as if they had not been staring at a set but sitting in a theatre, a cinema, a concert hall, a cabaret. So not a word that follows must be taken as unfriendly criticism of TV personnel. Good luck to you, boys and girls! Thanks a lot, Mary, Peter, Sylvia, Derek! But I am a Viewer too, one of the regular customers, even though I never ring up to complain that one of my precious prejudices has been ignored, and now I feel I must explain, as honestly as I know how, what the thing is doing to me.

The general line about TV—I took it myself before I became a Viewer—is that it is terrifically exciting, immensely powerful, potentially very dangerous. Here is this miraculous medium that pours into the home, hour after hour, night after night, images so dazzling and enticing that it immediately outbids all other media for its tenancy of the mind and imagination. It can transform any licence-holder into a well-informed and thoughtful student of all public affairs. It can turn children into future scholars of Trinity and Girton or into gunmen and molls. So we are playing with fire and dynamite—but what fire, what dynamite! This is the kind of stuff I wrote and talked myself before I became a real Viewer. Now that I know what happens, I can no longer write and talk in this strain. Certainly the medium produces its own particular effects, undoubtedly has an influence all its own; but these effects and this influence are very different from what they are generally imagined to be. Unless I am a very peculiar Viewer, the alarmists have all been looking in the wrong direction. They are like a man who expects a wolf at the door when he ought to be attending to the death watch beetle in the woodwork.

Instal a set, turn a switch—and hey presto!—here in a corner of the living-room is an ever-changing image of the whole wide, glittering, roaring world. Or so they say. But that is not quite how my viewing works. To begin with, it does not seem to bring the outside world closer to me but pushes it further away. There are times, after I have played the Lady of Shalott longer than usual, when this world is not here at all; I feel I am taking a series of peeps, perhaps from the darkened smoke room of a giant space-ship, at another planet, with whose noisy affairs I am not involved at all. Let me stare and idly listen long enough and I seem to have arrived at some theosophical astral-body-life-after-death. I am as little involved in or perturbed by all these conferences, departures and arrivals of shadowy Ministers, crashes and floods, strikes and lock-outs, aircraft and racing cars, atomic plants or fishing villages, scientists and film stars, as some Great White Master, a thousand years old, gazing into a crystal ball in Tibet. At most, these are—as one of Yeats's characters observed in another connection—the dreams the drowsy gods breathe on the burnished mirror of the world. I remember an old retired nannie, rather weak in the head, who when she visited the silent films thought everything she saw was part of one vast confused programme, an astonishing but acceptable mixture of the Prince of Wales and cowboys and Indians and Stanley Baldwin and sinking ships and *It*-girls and the Lord Mayor of London. She was an early Viewer. I know now exactly what she felt. Perhaps I am rather weak in the head too.

No sooner is any subject under review and discussion on the screen than it is drained of all reality. The instrument itself, probably guided by some satanic intelligence hostile to our species, adds a fatal dream effect. Even what I thought were urgent burning problems stop being problems at all. They are not settled, but their hash is. Somehow I no longer care what happens about Oil or Married Women At Work or Youth And The Churches Today or What We Do With The Old People or Whither Britain. I just view them. They might be bits from untidy and badly acted plays. Sometimes I don't know—and don't care—if the gesticulating image of a Foreign Minister belongs to a real Foreign Minister or to an actor in one of those political plays we are always having. Here on the screen the difference between Yugoslavia and Ruritania is hardly worth bothering about. After half-an-hour of The Future Of Our Fisheries or Africa At The Crossroads, the programme personalities, bursting with fisheries or Africa, stare accusingly at me and ask me what I propose to do about it. They might as well know now that, as a Viewer, I don't propose to do anything about it. After they have given me a final earnest look and asked their last question, I stare at the credit titles, listen dreamily to the end music, wonder idly why Malcolm Muggeridge looks handsomer on the screen than off, where Woodrow Wyatt has acquired his new haughty accent, light another pipe, and float into the next programme.

Perhaps it is *Picture Parade* or something of the sort, in which all the imbecilities of the film studio hand-outs and the fan magazines are given a kind of idiot dream life, especially—ah what golden moments!—in the foyer at a gala première where celebrities of screen and stage consent to smile at us and tell us how exciting it all is, as if we didn't know, and are wished lots of luck. As a Viewer I try not to miss one of these occasions. To view one, smoking in the darkened room with your feet up, is much better than actually being there, what with all the dressing up, the heat and fuss, the pushing and shoving to get nearer the mike or the Press photographers. It is a dream glimpse, carefully focused and timed, of a dream world. But it is all so *exciting*, as everybody keeps telling us Viewers. Perhaps that is why I so often find myself laughing—all alone, there in the dark—probably only a nervous excitement.

Some nights there seem to be dozens and dozens and dozens of people being interviewed, not just about films but about everything. We go all over the place—inside and outside Ministries, home and abroad, to airports and railway stations, to sports grounds and factories. The organisation of it all, the sheer technical achievements, are a credit to our civilisation. The courtesy and friendliness are admirable: all the persons interviewed are for ever being thanked and wished good luck. People under

Cabinet rank and sixty years of age are on Christian name terms at once. It is a wonderful and happy world, this of TV interviews. And perhaps that is why it is not a world in which anybody ever says anything. That might spoil it. Between the cordial *Hellos* and the charming *Good-byes* nothing much seems to happen. We are either going to the interview or coming away from it. "Let us," they say proudly, "go to Coketown and talk to the Mayor himself— so now *It's Over To Coketown*—This is Coketown and here in the studio is the Mayor of Coketown, who has kindly consented to talk to us—Very good of you, Mr. Mayor— er what about this er campaign of yours, Mr. Mayor?— Well, Reg, I think er I can say er we here in Coketown er hope to get it started fairly soon—Thank you, Mr. Mayor, and the best of luck—Thank you, Reg—And now we return you to London—This is London and that was the Mayor of Coketown being interviewed by our representative, Reg Rowbottom—and *now*——"

At first, when I was a new Viewer, a stranger in this magic world, I wanted the Mayor to say something, if only to justify all the trouble that had been taken to flash his image across the country. Now I know that this does not matter at all, that what is important is that we should keep jumping around, stare at a fresh face for a moment or two, then be off again. The instrument likes to do this, and it is the instrument that has us in its power. In this world of the magic tube, all the values are different. Here we are more interested in what the interviewer sounds and looks like than we are in what the interviewed person says. Viewing, I accept these topsy-turvy values. It is only afterwards, coming to my senses and thinking things over,

I begin to question them. Staring at the set, my mind almost a blank, I am quite ready to believe in TV personalities, the élite and aristocracy of this dream world. I do not ask what they have done, what massive talents they possess. They still have personalities where I, as a Viewer, a captive of the screen, have little or none. Not this Christmas but possibly the next, when I may have said good-bye to reality, I shall have no party of my own, perhaps will no longer understand what arrangements could be made for one; I will attend, as a Viewer, a party of TV personalities, to enjoy the sparkle of the wine in their glasses, to listen with joy to the crunching of their mince pies; and one or two of them may look straight in my direction, to wish me a Merry Christmas Programme, a Happy New Year's Viewing.

Meanwhile, sitting in the dark with my feet up, I feel I have *had* Fisheries or Africa or Youth And The Churches Today. I couldn't agree more about Married Women At Work or What We Do With The Old People or Whither Britain, and could hardly care less. We Viewers know now that we are such stuff as dreams are made on, that all is Maya, that *For in and out, above, below, 'Tis nothing but a magic shadow-show.* So it is easy to imagine oneself viewing the next war, dreamily watching whole cities crumble to radioactive dust, catching a last glimpse of Manchester or Leeds in between a thirty-minute detective play and some light music and a gipsy dancer. Never did a medium of information and entertainment arrive more opportunely, to soothe the tormented mind, to ease the bewilderment of the soul. We may emerge from our four or five years' bondage to it, having at last achieved detachment, for ever untroubled and smiling, finally victorious over the technique and the instrument. Already we Viewers, when not viewing, have begun to whisper to one another that the more we elaborate our means of communication, the less we communicate. Some words on a page can be unforgettable. The memory of an actor, moving and speaking on a platform, may haunt us all our lives. Then the inventors and technicians arrive, the costs rise prodigiously, the complication sets in, and we get film and radio, far less potent and memorable. The inventors and technicians, in a frenzy, with millions of money behind them, invade the home with TV, adding more and more images to sound, performing miracles with time and space, bringing in colour, stereoscopic sight, everything. And out of this mountain of invention and technique, finance and organisation, comes a little dream mouse. "Not bad," we Viewers cry. "What next?"

DR. LEAVIS

It seems that Dr. Leavis gave a lecture at Nottingham University on "Literature In My Time" and declared that apart from D. H. Lawrence there has been no literature in his time. He knocked hell out of everybody, and no doubt had all the Lucky Jims rolling down the aisles. Like Groucho Marx on another academic occasion, whatever it was he was against it. Virginia Woolf was a "slender talent"; Lytton Strachey "irresponsible and unscrupulous"; W. H. Auden "the career type", fixed at "the undergraduate stage"; Spender "no talent whatsoever"; Day-Lewis "Book Society author"; the whole age "dismal", and outlook "very poor". By the time Dr. Leavis caught his train back to Cambridge, there was hardly anything left to read in Nottingham. I have not the pleasure of the doctor's acquaintance—he was up at Cambridge just after me—but I have a vague but impressive vision of him, pale and glittering-eyed, shining with integrity, marching out of Downing to close whole departments of libraries, to snatch books out of people's hands, to proclaim the bitter truth that nobody writes anything worth reading. There is Lawrence; there is Leavis on Lawrence; perhaps a disciple, Jones, is writing something —let us say, Jones on Leavis on Lawrence; after that, nothing.

Years ago, just after he was appointed Chief Controller of Literary Passports, Dr. Leavis announced one morning

—playing for a laugh, for the boys and girls love this sort of thing—that no time need be wasted on Priestley. He was quite right too. Suppose a man said to me: "My boy's up at Cambridge doing English. It's a bit of a struggle for us to keep him there—that's why I've stopped smoking—so I don't want him to waste a minute of his time. Now, honestly, old man, do you think he ought to read your stuff?" I would reply without hesitation: "No, old man, he oughtn't. Leavis is quite right. If your boy's committed to *Eng. Lit.*, and at such a sacrifice too, he must be careful what he reads. But as we're being honest, old man, I must add one thing. For my part I wouldn't swap a pound of tobacco for all the *Eng. Lit.* courses in the country. If it's not too late, take your boy out of that mournful little racket, let him learn something while he has a chance."

It was about this time that Dr. Leavis, with one quick turn of the wrist, dropped most of the eighteenth century into the ash-can. No time need be wasted reading Fielding, Sterne, Goldsmith, Smollett. This seemed to some of us dabblers in letters to be rather severe. Sometimes I have wistfully tried to imagine a scene in Bow Street, with Dr. Leavis appearing before that formidable (though wise and compassionate) magistrate, Henry Fielding. For all his courage—and we must grant him that—Dr. Leavis, I suspect, would not cut a very impressive figure in the presence of Fielding. And with all due respect to this critic's integrity, and without any malice whatever, I cannot help feeling that whatever happened to him would serve him right. I am as vain, touchy, and aggressive as the next man—in fact, it is ten to one I am vainer, touchier, and more aggressive—but when I am considering a great personality and a massive original talent (probably the most precious thing in the world) I feel a little humility is not out of place. A Fielding may not be all he was once thought to be (I think he is, but that is not the argument), nevertheless he is still a whale of a fellow compared with anybody lecturing on literature at Cambridge. Literature is not well served when its giants are mutilated and slaughtered to fit a critical theory, here-today-and-gone-tomorrow. Nor are the intellectual manners of the young improved by the spectacle, offered them at an impressionable time, of such arrogant antics.

There could be, no doubt, a standard of literary values so high, so icily severe, that in its sight a Virginia Woolf would possess nothing but a slender talent. But from this height a Dr. Leavis would not exist at all. His loudest screams could never be heard. His claim to write even one sentence worth reading could not be accepted. This is where the arrogantly dogmatic, absolutist critic, behaving more like the Grand Inquisitor or Calvin than a sensible man of letters, walks into a trap. For if our time is so precious that we should not waste it reading a hundred reputable authors, from Fielding to Day-Lewis, then why should we waste any time reading or listening to Dr. Leavis? This question may not occur to undergraduates, who are impressed by fierce dogmatism, because they are themselves inclined towards intolerance, sweeping generalisations, knock-you-down judgments, hell-for-leather criticism, and sit up half the night opening bottles of beer and roaring this stuff at one another. So when Dr. Leavis tells his audiences that Mr. Auden has never advanced beyond the undergraduate stage, he should be careful, for his own success with undergraduates might be explained by the fact that his critical methods and temper have much in common with those of the average second-year man. It is the critic that is not conducting a permanent quarrel with everybody, that has sensible relative values, that does not divide writing into literature and rubbish, that knows that authors worth reading have many different virtues, who cannot have an easy success with undergraduates, just because he does not behave as they like to do, because he asks them to make an effort and civilise themselves.

The truth is that Dr. Leavis, though possibly an excellent teacher, is not really a literary critic at all. He is a sort of Calvinist theologian of contemporary culture. To be an author, in his view, is to invite damnation, for only a few—D. H. Lawrence, himself, and a favourite pupil or two—will be saved. The rest of us are not just a lot of chaps trying to get by, doing no particular harm to anybody, writing as well as we know how, but a gang of impudent or sinister charlatans, probably sitting up at night plotting against him. The very title of his critical journal, *Scrutiny*, suggests that in it authors will have to undergo some kind of customs and passport examination, that the editor and his contributors will be there with narrowed gaze, tight lips, service revolvers. *Scrutiny* may have vanished, but Dr. Leavis and his disciples are still on the job scrutinising, refusing bribes, closing the frontier to all the scribbling riffraff. Even when he produces an enthusiastic study of Lawrence, which contains some admirable chapters, he forfeits our sympathy by behaving as if he were conducting a scholarship examination for a single place, as if the writing of fiction were entirely competitive, as if you cannot pass Lawrence without failing Arnold Bennett or Mr. Forster. He makes one feel that he hates books and authors, that his astonishing severity does not come from exceptional fastidiousness but is the result of some strange neurosis, as if he had been frightened by a librarian in early childhood. His solemnity is not the usual donnish conceit, from which he is free, but suggests the neurotic theologian. He is an unusual man, with genuine gifts, hard and passionately at work on the wrong job.

For the last twenty-five years, both here and in America, especially in the universities, bad criticism has been driving out good criticism. It is always absolutist, never relative. Either something is literature, we are told, or it isn't. There are no innumerable fine shades between very great writing, at one end of the scale, and silly nonsense at the other. Everything is all or nothing. There is only one kind of excellence, one set of literary virtues. If Smith is in, then Brown is out. Whatever it cannot praise with solemn rapture, this criticism instantly and intolerantly abuses. It exists in an atmosphere that has the sour smell of fanaticism. Nobody is having any fun there, except the torturers in the basement. The bad critic has no sense of proportion about books and authors, and not much more about himself. He has an air of immense *hauteur*, is elaborately condescending and disdainful, and his favourite weapon is the mysterious sneer. (Of which "Book Society author" is typical. What has been said here worth saying? Nothing.) He insults and patronises men and women who may not be original geniuses but at least have learnt how to write, which is more than most of these critics have done. He never seems to be addressing ordinary sensible readers, men and women of the world, as the great critics always did, but only an elect few, a shadowy élite, for whom alone Literature exists.

So although I enjoy my vision of little Doc. Leavis slugging away, with the lecture hall a red ruin of literary reputations, truth compels me to add that I think he and his kind, in universities both here and in America (where the doctor has considerable influence), have done much mischief to the art they are boarded and lodged to serve. They catch the young, whose natural intolerance they do nothing to correct, at an impressionable age, and either turn them into equally bad critics or make them feel they want nothing more to do with literature. At a time when honest good writing is fighting for its life, with all the odds mounting up against it, they and their disciples are doing little to help and much to hinder. They are not bringing life to letters, letters to life. They are overlooking the important fact that, in the world outside universities, reading is not a compulsory activity. They are not sending into it young men and women with sound tastes and reasonable judgment, capable of writing a good book or two and of appreciating all that is worth enjoying. A man who tells a crowd of youngsters that literature in his time consists of D. H. Lawrence and nothing else but slender talents and trashy mountebanks may give the boys and girls an uproariously good evening, flattering the raw destructive element in the young; but he is not behaving like a genuine critic of literature, like a sensible teacher, like a man with any real concern for the culture of his time. The outlook may be "very poor"; I suspect that it is; but the firework displays of neurotic egoism will not light us very far on the way. Come, come; you have excellent qualities —and they have been widely acknowledged, even by those of us to whom you allow nothing—so do not misuse them, Dr. Leavis.

PUBLISHERS

I hope this piece will not be dishonest. While I was in South America, I was turned into a publisher, becoming a director of the re-organised Bodley Head. (Please note I am not a very active director and no manuscripts should be sent to me.) Thirty-five years ago, just down from Cambridge, I became a reader for the Bodley Head, the last that John Lane himself ever had. It is worth remembering that this successful and once very fashionable publisher first arrived in London as a railway clerk from a village in North Devon. This was remarkable in those bad old days, but now, of course, railway clerks are becoming successful fashionable publishers all the time. Anyhow, just as I joined the Bodley Head on my way in, now that I am on my way out, I join it again. But as I have not yet attended a Board Meeting, perhaps I can keep this piece reasonably honest.

Before we take a look at the book trade, let us agree to ignore the statistics, swollen with the vast traffic in things like *Easy Commercial Spanish* and *How to Clean a Motorcycle*. We are not concerned here with the writing, publication, wholesale and retail sale of such stuff. I do not even believe that much of it helps to subsidise the publication of literature. What it chiefly does is to bedevil the statistics and to confuse us.

Considering the genuine book trade, I do not find that

the publisher cuts a very sinister figure in it. I think of him as a friend rather than as an enemy. Most of the publishers I know seem to me, even now in these tough times, to be on the side of good books and good authors. They are anxious to publish what appears to them to be literature. They may not build up lists with the loving care displayed by publishers fifty years ago, may not be able to keep good authors going year after year at a loss as they used to do, but they have not entirely broken with their best traditions. Most of them know that if it is simply money you are after, it is idiotic to be a publisher at all—better to sell sausages or soap. They have a genuine liking for books, and although they may grumble about authors, they are proud to be associated with all but the worst of them.

When I go abroad and meet publishers there, I do not instantly feel that I am in touch with men superior to those I know in London. And this is in sharp contrast to what I feel when I visit bookshops abroad, where they appear to belong to a newer and better civilisation than ours. Even a good bookshop in this country seems to be clinging to what remains of literature like a man hanging on a cliff, whereas the shops abroad, spacious and attractive, nobly stocked and intelligently served, suggest that literature is one of the chief concerns of society. These shops also suggest that there exists all round them a large intelligent reading public, served in its turn by newspapers and periodicals that take writers and writing seriously. There is a further suggestion that even in the official national life of these countries the author has his own place.

(Recently, I was in the South of Chile, among the lakes and volcanoes, when the Chilean national poet, Gabrielle Mistral, was given an official funeral, a thousand miles away, and even down there flags everywhere were being flown at half-mast. If the whole Council of the Society of Authors here dropped dead next week, not a flag would be out at half-mast; and the news, unless we had all been poisoned, would not make the front page.)

When, therefore, I return from abroad, it is not the publishers I regard with dismay. Indeed, I may regard them with a new respect, realising how little encouragement they receive, how shabby the whole environment of the trade seems here, how strange it is that a country like ours, so rich in literary tradition, should make the publication and sale of literature so difficult. (What influence, what malignant spirit, is it that hates good writing and would like to banish it from our society?) There are moments when publishers begin to look like wine merchants in Mecca.

Nevertheless—and at the risk of being banned from that Board before I have ever taken my seat at it—I will venture some criticism of these gallant fellows, imperfect as we all are. They are not without sins of both commission and omission. My respect, warm with admiration, cannot blind me to these faults and failures.

First, I would have them remember, not when they are planning their social life but when they are behind closed doors working out costs, that publishing rests upon the author. No authors, no publishing. And authors, like paper-makers, printers, binders, and the rest, are here up to the neck in our inflationary society; the butchers and grocers and tobacconists do not make special rates for authors; and whatever it is that compels the paper-makers, printers, binders, to ask for more is also hard at work on the authors, making them wish they could ask for more too. But all too often the author, on whom the whole business really rests, is treated as the one soft spot on the budget. If the hard-faced boys want more, then take something away from soft-face, who will never go on strike or refuse to supply his goods and services. This is not well, gentlemen. It is far removed from that feeling about authors which first took you into a publishing house.

Next, in common with other people in the book trade, publishers seem to have made little or no attempt to grapple with the economic changes in our post-war society. Now in many a middle-class home, as we have heard the publishers and booksellers lament, there is no longer the money for buying books. That cannot be helped. But a mile away, down some dingy little street, there are some working-class homes, with three or four wage-earners, where there is plenty of spare money, but none of it is being spent on books. There is, of course, no bookshop anywhere near the street, and the idea of visiting the distant one in the Market Square does not occur to anybody. But by this time the trade might have devised a few notions for getting books into that street, for encouraging some people to buy books who never thought of it before. And I do not merely think that publishers have been at fault here, I *know* they have. When, just over a year ago, I broached this subject on television, most publishers were not even mildly interested.

Again, though I appreciate publishing difficulties due

to rising costs, I am absolutely opposed to the new demands being made by publishers for an increasingly larger share of authors' subsidiary rights—*e.g.*, dramatic, film, radio, and TV rights, as well as book club and second serial and other literary rights. The argument runs as follows: it costs more and more to publish a book and the publisher may easily lose money on it; if then the author makes money out of these subsidiary rights, the publisher is entitled to a good share of that money, because if it had not been for his capital and enterprise nobody would have heard of the author and his book. Now, in the first place, this is clearly not true of many authors, who do not need publishers to bring them into touch with the theatre, films, radio, and TV. And although, for example, a very successful novel may command far more money for one or other of these rights, if it has been so successful the publisher has already recouped himself handsomely, out of his own business, which is where he should make his money. Indeed, one of the chief objections to this sharing of rights, whether in publishing, the theatre, or elsewhere, is that it encourages men to neglect their own business in the hope of making money out of somebody else's.

We are told that more and more small publishing houses are coming under the financial control of the large houses. I see no harm in this so long as the small publisher still has editorial freedom. Indeed, it might help to put an end to the overproduction of books. For we have had too many publishers, all anxious to have something that looked like a list. This has resulted in the publication of too many books that nobody really cared about, books hacked out of other books, third-rate biographies, dim travel, tedious reminiscences, lending-library fodder, all of them getting in the way of real books, cluttering up catalogues and counters. And any move that reduces this sort of publishing has my support.

A last thought. It seems to me that publishers should entertain far more than they do at present, for I am under the impression that there is nothing like the literary hospitality there was in London before the war, and publishers are better able to provide this hospitality than authors are. It is entirely to their advantage that the authors they publish, especially the newcomers, should meet other authors, and that something like literary society should still exist in London. People concerned with the writing, publication, and sale of good books, as distinct from war memoirs, flash-in-the-pan adventure yarns, and the autobiographies of 'TV personalities', should form ranks and then begin to close them. In this country, it seems, the art of writing makes fewer and fewer friends and apparently more and more enemies. Most of the publishers I know are by no means indifferent to this art, and genuinely wish to serve it. Let them then try and rally us moody fellows, dine and wine us out of our mutual mistrust, encourage us to form a few combative alliances before we are all separately hunted down and carted off to old men's homes and mental institutions.

THE WRITER IN A
CHANGING SOCIETY

In the title of this lecture the writer comes first, perhaps to attract the customers. But in the lecture itself we must first examine and consider, however briefly and inadequately, our changing society before we can arrive at the writer's place in it. This will not be easy, but rather like trying to do a running commentary on the croquet game in *Alice in Wonderland* where hoops, balls, mallets, had an independent life of their own. We are so close to many of these changes, so much involved in some of them, that it is impossible for us to estimate their size, force, and importance. Many people get rid of this challenge by pretending it isn't there; they keep running away from the facts, a form of sport in which we English still excel. Thus it is wrong, in my view, to suppose that we are recovering from the last war, that we are still living in the society we once knew, merely with some economic and social changes giving it a turn here, a twist there. It is ironical that those of us who believe our society has been—and is being—profoundly changed, who try to understand what is really happening, who ask where we are going, should be so often accused of merely lamenting the vanished past. To us there is no sting in the taunt: "This is the future you wanted; now you regret the past." We know that behind our re-cognition of these profound changes, behind our criticism of what is virtually a new society, is still the same concern about the future: we are asking again "Where are we going?" And this question is not answered by announcements that we may be going to the moon in plastic spacesuits. It is indeed an awkward question, and to ask it is to take a short cut to public disapproval in many quarters. One encounters so much queer resistance, so much immediate loss of temper, so much surprising discourtesy and downright personal abuse, that it is hard not to believe that a great many English writers and readers are struggling to suppress a deep-seated irrational fear of the contemporary situation. You are often accused of deliberately darkening your view, giving yourself up to a sour distaste for your time, merely because you recognise and comment upon the facts of this situation. But it is the false optimist, shouting down any suggestion that we are not halfway to paradise, who has the blackest pessimism in his heart, having secretly abandoned himself to despair. It is the man who refuses to believe that life is a rat-trap who risks asking the awkward questions; he is not terrified by the prospect of having them answered. And unless we know where we are, how can we know where we are going? All summer in the Isle of Wight there go roaring down our narrow roads certain motor coaches boldly and hopefully labelled *Mystery Tour*. Although we still talk of planning, although we read about what we shall wear and how we shall travel in the future, the popular view is that our society now rides on the front seat of a *Mystery Tour*. This may help to explain why so many people believe in flying saucers coming from outer space; they are hoping secretly that at least these little blue creatures from Venus know where we are going.

I repeat, to have this sensible concern about the future, to keep on asking, not unreasonably: "Where are we going?" is to cut now an odd and disturbing figure. We are no longer living in a society where this question is always being asked, where this outlook is widely accepted. Vision has been replaced by television. Many of you will be surprised—and all of you will be immensely relieved—when I announce, as I do now, that this will not be a political address. Nevertheless, politics cannot be entirely omitted from a discussion of our society. And nobody can deny that our political climate has changed. At one time, not so long ago, it was the custom at Tory meetings to sing 'Rule, Britannia' and at Labour meetings to struggle through Blake's 'Jerusalem'. I hope both practices have been discontinued, for it is as absurd to be asked to imagine Mr. Butler ruling the waves as it is to imagine Mr. Gaitskell, being in receipt of the bow of burning gold he indented for, proceeding to build Jerusalem in England's green and pleasant land. Both parties rightly argue about the tax on babies' bootees, but neither party seems to know or care what kind of society will welcome the babies when they have grown out of these bootees. It is essentially short-term politics, with the struggle for immediate power naked and unashamed. The difference between Blue and Red has to be discovered in the black-and-white of the weekly reviews. The revolutionary impulse, whether to re-create a Merrie Old England or to build a wonderful new one, inspires neither the speakers nor their dwindling audiences. The packed hall has been replaced by the television performance, unsuitable for either visionary eloquence or philosophical argument, chiefly depending for its success on entertainment value and an apparently frank appeal to the viewers' immediate self-interest. Politics on this low level may be preferable to former kinds; that is beside my present point, which is that there has been a great change in our political climate.

The politicians have changed; so have the electorate. Millions have arrived at what seems so far to be security; they have full employment; they work shorter hours for a great deal more money. Let me add here that I for one do not regret these changes in themselves, though I do feel that too many of them have taken place in the wrong atmosphere, in which too often people were bought off rather than rewarded for zest, skill, and a heightened sense of responsibility; and in which the materials needed for the expansion or even the repair of the nation's cultural life had last place in any list of priorities. Perhaps Governments have had too many economists advising them, and might have consulted with advantage a psychologist and a social philosopher or two. For example, we have heard a great deal about the economic pros and cons of inflation, but nobody in authority points out that it is bad just because it soon turns so many people into money-chasers, with lower and lower standards of personal integrity, all in a rat race. We should remember too—especially those of us who had the luck to start in an easier time—that inflation creates appalling difficulties for the young writer. Forty-five years ago I sold my first article to a London periodical, and I received a guinea for it. That seems poor pay until you remember, as I do, that you could rent a well-built stone cottage near the moors for ninepence a week, keep yourself in food for ten shillings, cover your week's supply of tobacco (at fourpence an ounce) and beer (at tuppence a pint) with another three or four shillings. Again, we are now recommended—I heard a well-known industrial scientist hard at it, the other day, on the air—to adopt completely what I have called elsewhere the *Admass* system. Production goes up and up because high-pressure advertising and salesmanship constantly create new needs that must be satisfied: this is *Admass*—a consumers' race with donkeys chasing an electric carrot. This enables you to build up and enjoy a civilisation in which innumerable men with anxiety neuroses sit cursing in new and larger cars that cannot move, just because innumerable other men, with stomach ulcers, are also out in their new and larger cars. In *Admass* you press on with your particular swindle in order to have more money to spend on other men's swindles. Much of this elaborate folly is the result of thinking in terms of figures, statistics, abstractions, and not in terms of human beings and their age-old primary satisfactions, for which three visits a week to a psycho-analyst are a poor substitute. And it is where this vast ant-hill idiocy is triumphant that people can spend more and more money making gigantic bombs and exploding them; and—let us note in passing—where society is less and less concerned about its authors and its literature.

It has been suggested that this sudden and massive improvement in the standard of living, for so many millions, is now creating a new middle class, to replace perhaps an older disappearing one. But the point about a middle class—and the secret of its value and importance—is that it is in the middle. It does not want the direct enjoyment of power itself, but on the other hand it does not feel itself to be so materially insecure that it will gladly barter liberty for security. It can afford to be sharply suspicious of all concentrations of power. Its middle position, where it is neither manipulating nor being manipulated by the power system, leaves it free to feel a certain responsibility, perhaps personal to each member and yet traditional in the class, about society in general, keeping in mind certain broad values, asking the awkward questions and if necessary announcing unpopular answers. Nonsense about the *bourgeois*—and, let us admit, an occasional atmosphere too thick with comfort and complacency—should not blind us to the fact that generally it is from this class in the middle that our arts and revolutionary ideas have come. But the new middle class cannot be expected to have these advantages and virtues because in fact it is not in the middle. It wants—and I am not blaming it—security at almost any cost. It is not suspicious of any great concentration of power. It feels no responsibility for the state of society in general, knows no reason why it should make any sacrifice to keep certain values alive, is not concerned about those values. Naturally it has no such tradition, newly released as it is from the grinding pressure of circumstance, determined to enjoy, as most of us would in the same position, its new freedom from material want. It follows no revolutionary gleam, asks for none to follow, because its Jerusalem is here, complete with greyhound tracks, football grounds, ice shows, dance halls, cinemas, sports finals, another sensational story next Sunday, and television personalities. The show is in full swing. And things that once had reality for the mind, meaning for the heart, begin to be part of the show:

loyalty and patriotism are processions and parades; religion is Billy Graham at Harringay; and even in cricket and football we now have the slow handclap, telling the players that the audience—no longer their devoted followers, cheering them to conquest, but just an audience —is not amused. There is now a vast crowd that is a permanent audience waiting to be amused, cash customers screaming for their money's worth, all fixed in a consumer's attitude. They look on at more and more, and join in less and less.

We are told we are too impatient; we must allow a little more time for education to do its work. I try to accept this argument; knowing myself to be impatient, I submit meekly to any rebuke it contains. Moreover, I am the son of a schoolmaster, who had for education a greater passion than most people now have for anything. But education best succeeds when the whole environment of the child or youth is in its favour. There will always be born scholars, of course, but we are not discussing them. With ordinary youngsters, if the home is against the school, the home will win; if what happens in the street contradicts what is taught in school, the street will win. On the other hand, if the home and the street play the right part, some later years of schooling, except for purely technical education, can be dispensed with. I know this from experience, for between the time I left school and then went to a university there was a gap of several years, during which I pretended to work in a wool office; but because I was fortunate in my home, my town, my time, I believe I developed more in those years than in any others. But then when I left school a lad could pick up the nearest

newspaper and learn something, as I did from the intellectual high spirits of Chesterton, the superb descriptive
prose of H. M. Tomlinson. True, as many of our friends
engaged in further education point out to us, there are
even more opportunities now for youngsters to cultivate
their minds: they have only to join one of a thousand
classes, buy a paper-backed book, turn the right switch on
the wireless set. But these optimistic enthusiasts overlook
the fact that other and quite different enterprises have
now developed even faster still. They under estimate the
growth and relentless pressure of mass communications,
and the power wielded by those that manipulate them.
Mass persuasion, using all the technical devices of the new
age, is now a giant industry, served by armies of highly
paid experts and with stupendous sums of money invested
in it. Any plan to maintain and assert good values will be
lucky if it can find a thousand pounds. Offer to seduce the
innocent on behalf of shoddy values, and you can raise
millions. And unfortunately this is a time when it is increasingly difficult for small and very personal enterprises
to succeed at all; they are like protesting ordinary human
voices being raised, at the back of a giant cinema, against
the bellowing and roaring apparently coming from the
mouths on the screen, mouths four feet wide at least and in
glorious technicolour. Yet, in spite of all this evil enchantment, are not Shakespeare, Rembrandt, Beethoven, still
with us, sometimes even served by these machines of mass
culture? They are indeed—and we thank God for it. They
and their like may yet win through, just because there is in
them something indestructible that cannot fail to attract
to itself something unconquerable in the human spirit.

But we should remember, if only to keep ourselves vigilant, that our age may be drawing on a spiritual cultural capital, accumulated by past generations, and that if we continue to move as fast as we have been doing recently, we may soon be in a position where we can neither deposit nor withdraw any more: the very bank may be out of sight and out of mind.

Anything may happen; and I for one am no better qualified to be a prophet of the future than I am to be a historian of the past. But we do appear to be on the point of achieving, if we have not already arrived at it, a new society. It will be a society without that old middle class, deprived therefore of the outlook of the better members of that class, the vigilant, combative, radical, and enthusiastic persons, already disappearing from the scene. It will consist largely of small groups enjoying the exercise of power, and a great mass, no longer haunted by the images of any bows of burning gold and arrows of desire, content to be ordered about and moulded so long as it feels materially secure, comfortable, and not too bored for lack of amusement. At work or at play it will not be asked to make any great effort. More and more it will live vicariously, at secondhand: enjoying the rich gaudy life its favourites lead; being indignant with the morning paper, being complacent with the evening one; enjoying romance and passionate love through its film stars; being jovial, charming, or rude through its television personalities. Those who are not satisfied with existence on this level, who want sharper flavours, higher rewards, who are not afraid of responsibility, who would rather manipulate than be manipulated, will take care to climb one of the ladders of power, erected by the government departments, public corporations, trade unions, industrial empires, organisations for mass communications, that will rule this society. They will do their climbing, I fancy, carefully, smoothly, without much self-assertion, being anxious to avoid any suspicion that they are not sound co-operative fellows. The men and women who express their dissatisfaction with the mass level not by climbing out of it but by open rebellion against it will probably be regarded as dangerous anti-social types in need of corrective psychological treatment. For this will be a society that is closing in and not opening out, reversing the whole movement of the nineteenth and early twentieth centuries. The former rebels, nonconformists, breakers away, namely the scientists and the technocrats, will now be the authoritarians. It will be largely their society, created by them, maintained by them. It might easily appear to be the dream-come-true of our friend H. G. Wells, though I am certain he would hate it, just because so much he loved—and of course mistakenly assumed would always be there—would have to be dropped out on the way. Kipling—the Kipling of *As Easy As A.B.C.*—comes nearer to being its prophet than the humorous, zestful, life-loving, eternally rebellious H. G. Risking a moment's prophecy myself, I will venture to declare that even were such a society to be firmly established for some generations, it could not endure long. It would be based on too narrow a conception of man's fundamental nature, of what his mind and soul require, and so would either soon run down, losing even its own skills in a growing listlessness, boredom, yawning satiety, or explode, from the sheer force of what had been driven into the unconscious and allowed to rot there, and end in appalling violence, cruelty, mad chaos. For what is deepest in our being cannot be long defied or ignored: God is not mocked.

Let me make haste now to remove any hint of Science Fiction from this lecture, and return to today. Are there any signs that such a new society might be almost within sight? I think so, though I admit that in a time of rapid change it is easy to pick out the signs you require as proof, ignoring others that are no help to you. But all the recent changes, political, economic, social, cultural, we have already briefly noted seem to point in one direction. And is there not about many of the young now an air of conformity, not an eager and zestful air, no suggestion of having enlisted in a crusade, but one that produces either a smooth, bland, faintly cynical manner, in the apprentice politician or official, or a somewhat loutish style of sullen acquiescence, found in some younger novelists? And no revolutionary ardour, on behalf of any possible kind of changed England; no open rebellion, not even out of youthful high spirits; just shoulder-shrugging, umbrella-rolling, and the assembling of references in triplicate to be posted to the right address. In a financial advertisement I saw the other day, a young man was shown asking an older man about a job, and he was saying, this new Elizabethan: "Does it carry a pension?" Of course there are plenty of lively exceptions to all this safe planning and careful conformity, but we are observing the general drift among the educated. And perhaps these cautious young men know instinctively—what some of us elders are beginning to feel—that ours is a society that is no longer opening out, as it did for generation after generation: it is closing in. If you listen hard, you can hear the doors being quietly closed—sometimes, keys being turned. This is the land and the era of the smooth administrator, the good man with a committee, who will never put a foot wrong even if he never puts a hand right. Even in enterprises and institutions connected with scholarship and the arts, more and more the key positions are not filled by scholars or artists but by retired men of action, political throw-outs, or professional administrators, rather as if the rest of us were old natives of a Crown Colony. Time after time we find the preference given to the negative type, even when the job may cry out for a positive, creative man: as if no premises could be insured if the man in charge has fire in his belly. If all this is too vague and you need a concrete example, here is one of some interest to us writers. What kind of men should direct, at the very top, such enterprises as television and sound radio? I reply without hesitation: "Why, men who are mad, out of their minds with blazing enthusiasm, about television and sound radio, who are certain that these are the most fascinating, rewarding, inspiring media the world has ever known, who brood over them all day and dream about them all night, who are ready to kill you if you don't do your damnedest, but if you show yourself worthy of using this miraculous medium will fall on your neck and summon, in a voice of thunder, delectable damsels to bring you champagne and old brandy. Those are the men who should be at the very top, in the very centre, of such organisations, with administrators, ten a penny, ranking far below them— artists, madmen, visionaries, creators, not men who'd

hardly notice the difference if they found themselves
moved to the Board of Trade. Certainly, with these
blazing enthusiasts in charge, mistakes would be made,
whole programmes would be wrecked, whole cities left
feeling outraged—and why not?—they wouldn't be
running a train service; there are art and life in these
things somewhere, and such men would blow them into a
flame. Does anybody imagine that the Viennese Opera,
the Moscow Art Theatre, the Boston Symphony, were
created and then perfected by sound administrative types,
appointed by twaddling, yawning committees, who would
wake up and send for the police if a man of genius appeared
before them?" (End of concrete example and dramatic
interlude.)

Am I mistaken in thinking that during the last few years
the people who have the real power have begun dropping
old quarrels, are discovering they have much in common,
and seem to be quietly moving nearer one another, not
quite consolidating yet but perhaps achieving a new and
valuable understanding? Am I being fanciful—it is a
weakness of mine—if I seem to discover a widening gap
between members of these power groups and the great
anonymous mass of our fellow citizens, staring at the headlines, switching on their sets? Would I be wrong in appear-
to detect a more obvious and blatant cynicism among
those in the know? Are other people noticing how one
kind of crowd manipulator and hoodwinker is now quickly
supported and encouraged by other kinds? Or how
almost all the awkward questions are either ignored or
hastily silenced, often by loud abuse of the questioner, who
is not worth listening to because he is too Red, too Blue,

too revolutionary, too reactionary, too rich, too poor, too anything, too nothing? Are we right in thinking that a large section of our Press now is not so much sensational as determinedly and unblushingly trivial, like a nurse amusing an idiot child? Am I alone in believing that all this evidence seems to point one way, towards a new pattern of society quite different from the one we read about in little books, chiefly meant for export, on the British Way of Life? Sometimes I have felt that we catch a glimpse of what is really happening to us, a glimpse far more revealing than anything offered to us in the little books, when we attend, see, or hear about—of all things—the occasion known as a gala film première. Such functions seem to be a kind of caricature, in motion and brilliantly illuminated, of our recent social developments and changes, the pattern of tomorrow's society. There, waiting in the drizzle and the outer darkness, is the huge, nameless, faceless mob, pressing against the cordons of police, good-humoured enough as persons no doubt, but in its collective capacity, as a mob, capable one night of something outrageous and horrifying. Incidentally, there is a memorable and frightening account of such a mob in Hollywood at the end of a novel called *The Years of the Locust*. Then, within the brilliantly lighted area surrounded by the police, arriving in their massive noiseless motors, are the privileged guests of the evening, the aristocracy of the new order, men of power—for there may be Cabinet Ministers, high officials, wealthy industrialists, newspaper magnates, and the like—and the glamorous darlings of the watching crowd, the film stars, TV personalities, entertainers, the wit and beauty of the gossip columns, all moving magnificently towards the blazing foyer, as the flash-bulbs explode, the cameras turn, the microphones crackle into life, to record these shining moments for millions not able to join the crowd outside. And among those millions there are probably several thousand pretty girls and clever young men who realise, perhaps in despair, perhaps with re- newed determination, that here, brilliant on the screen, roaring through the loudspeaker, is their goal, the high peak of ambition, the summit of achievement. I have put one of them, a young provincial girl with ambition and dreams, in my comedy *Mr. Kettle and Mrs. Moon*, and audiences seem to find her very funny. But she is only giving them what they accept, without protests or jeers, from most of their newspapers every day. These youngsters, you will tell me, are very foolish. I agree. But are they any more foolish than some of their solemn elders who assume that our society and its values have remained unchanged? Are they not perhaps less dangerously off the mark?

On the occasion I have described, it is possible—for somebody had to write the film they are going to see—that an author or two might be present, looking as we do on all such occasions—not very impressive, rather crumpled. We would hardly expect an author to cut much of a figure at a function of this kind. We no longer—mistakenly perhaps—aim at the sort of appearance, the type of persons, that would achieve instant and delighted re- cognition from the crowd. Bernard Shaw could do it of course, after working hard at it for many years, but then Shaw was essentially a Victorian and Edwardian. The truth is—the author does not cut a much more impressive figure in the society represented, even if caricatured, by the gala opening. Take that film they are going to see, for example. The man who wrote it ought to be regarded as one of its creators—indeed, as the magical being who first conjured the tale it tells out of the air—but you may safely accept long odds that his place in the studio hierarchy is a modest one, a little above that of the chief make-up man but below the cameraman. In the film industry the author has never been seriously regarded as the creator, the artist, the prophet, the originating genius, whose vision of life all must serve. At times he may have been praised and even petted, he has often been generously rewarded; but his actual status in the studios has generally been that of a superior technician. And here, I think, television has largely followed film practice. It is not the writers for television who take up so much space in the daily Press. And it is this actual status that has lately been frankly recognised by my friends and colleagues in the Screenwriters Association, who, at a meeting not long ago, passed a resolution by an overwhelming majority that previously they had rejected with equal force: a resolution to turn the Association into a trades union, which would be affiliated to the other unions of studio workers. They felt compelled—and I am not blaming them—for the sake of reasonable security to acknowledge that they were technicians within the machinery of film or TV production, and not creative artists for whose sake it was set in motion. This action seems to me symbolic. The writer is finding his place in a changing society.

I shall be told that films and television are, after all, off the centre as far as authorship is concerned. Possibly they are, though they are not off the centre so far as our society is concerned; anything that children and young people find magically compelling, almost hypnotic, must sooner or later have a social influence and importance hard to exaggerate. Authors may have some share of that influence and importance, but, as we have already seen, they will have to claim it not as artists but as superior technicians, largely working within the machinery of production. In these new and powerful media, so typical of our era in the brilliance of their know-how and the poverty of their know-why, the living writer must accept a lower status or keep out. I say *living* writer because there may long be some acceptance of and perfunctory homage to dead writers, whose works can be cut and trimmed, whose mouths are stopped. You never quite know what a living writer will say next, though if you can make him punch a time clock at the studio gate you probably won't have to worry too much about that. Some authors might batter their way through and still insist upon the machine serving them and their individual vision of things, but the odds against those heroes are rapidly lengthening. Such an assault, such a reversal of mass media values, depends partly on the authors' combative will and partly on their prestige. And if their prestige is dwindling, if the magic of their names is fading, then it will be safer to clock in with the other union men. The writer as superior technician will survive. But the author in his older and larger capacities, as a unique individual and yet a truly representative figure of his time, may not survive. The new society, when it has closed its ranks and completed its arrangements, will hardly have room for him. He is already being served notice to quit.

Here we must steady ourselves to meet the impact of a simple brutal attack upon our whole position. "You say," the objector tells us, his eyes glittering with malice, "that the prestige and status of authorship are declining, and you're ready to discover some pretty fancy reasons for this decline. But aren't you overlooking the obvious reason? There used to be giants, now there are dwarfs, and the public isn't blind—y'know, old boy." This objection is easily answered. It may be that the England of my youth, before the First War, was magnificently rich in literary talent; indeed, I happen to believe that this brief period, blown to bits by the war, was one in which a peculiarly English genius flowered exquisitely in several arts. We may indeed be dwarfs to their giants. But there were earlier decades—the one, for example, that greeted with such relief and enthusiasm the appearance of the young Kipling—in which for a time dwarfs were assumed to be giants, so high and magical was the prestige of authorship, so determined was the public to have great literary figures. Again, when I am in London I live in Albany and every time I go in and out I pass a bust of Bulwer-Lytton. Now one of my neighbours there is Mr. Grahame Greene, and so far, I think, no plans have been made by the Albany landlords to secure a bust of him. I do not happen to share Mr. Greene's vision of this life, but of one thing I am certain—he is a much better novelist than Bulwer-Lytton ever was. And if only to keep in character, I will add that I am a much better dramatist than he ever was. But let us avoid both literary criticism and boasting, even though I have some capacity for both. The point is—that even if we are dwarfs following giants, this has happened before in English letters, during the last hundred and fifty years, without the consequences and developments I am sketching tonight. No matter whether we are good, bad, or indifferent authors, we are not responsible for what is happening. As our society changes its structure, outlook, character, tone, atmosphere, so the relation between it and our profession changes too—and, in my view, rapidly for the worse.

But books? Never mind television and films and that sort of thing—look at the books! Why, this is the very time of year when the publishers are sending them out, the booksellers taking them in, by the ton. There are far too many new books published now: everybody says so. This is true. To be brutally frank, there are too many publishers concocting lists because they cannot be publishers without lists. With the result, even if we leave out purely educational and technical volumes, that nine-tenths of these books can safely be ignored here; they are just book trade merchandise. And if we begin to ask a few searching questions, the whole booklovers' fancy fair begins to look rather shabby. Here are some. How many small publishing houses, with no standard lines to support them, and with a concern for the literary quality of their lists, are paying their way? How many individual booksellers, men who really care about books, are doing well? One told me the other day he was in despair. How many good writers —not geniuses but men and women well worth reading— are finding themselves with decreasing incomes, at a time when everybody else is demanding and receiving more and more? How many authors have agreed to take serious cuts in their percentages for royalties? What has happened to their incomes from magazines and newspapers? Yes, money. For once let us talk about money. I say "for once" because for thirty years I have read highly satirical accounts by comic writers of literary parties at which authors talk about nothing but sales, royalties, money; and in thirty years I have never attended one of these parties and indeed have no idea of the sales, royalties, incomes, of my oldest and closest friends who are writers. But we do at times perceive some lack of proportion in things. Some years ago I was in Toronto and recorded some talks for the radio there. When I asked about payment, I was told to remember that Canada was still a new country, struggling along in comparative poverty, so I mustn't expect much. I said: "This morning I paid the equivalent of twelve-and-six for a Canadian haircut. Now make up your mind what you are, please. If you're a twelve-and-sixpenny haircut country, then pay me properly for my talks. If you're too poor to do that, then knock eleven shillings off the haircut." The trouble is, it is not only the innocent, who write and ask us for six copies of our books for remote bazaars, who seem to imagine that we authors really live on the moon or in the Forest of Arden. Publishers, editors, and the like, all tell us we must take less because everything is costing more and more, just as if somehow we were outside these price pressures, as if at the sight of us the butcher and baker burst into tears and refused to take a penny. Now, to play fair, I will offer two estimated figures of my own. If, taking into account the purchasing power of money, my remuneration were on the same scale as it was twenty-five years ago, my royalty now on a long novel would be about eight shillings a copy. Earlier than that, as a young critic, not at that time a successful novelist, I did a weekly article on books for the *Evening News*; and to be paid equally well now for the same work —and this is not taking tax into account, only the value of the pound—I would have to be given well over a hundred pounds an article. And any young critic today who is looking for this rate of payment should forget about books, learn how to play an instrument, to paint his face, and to sing lyrics in praise of soap flakes.

If our money goes down while nearly everybody else's goes up—moreover, in a society in which more and more people are involved cosily in pension, superannuation, endowed insurance schemes, while we have the bleak prospect of a Civil List pension of two hundred a year—it is not merely because we may be soft bargainers but because the iron law of supply and demand is against us. The society that began opening out, early in the nineteenth century, raised our status as authors; the society that is changing so quickly now, and seems to be closing in, is cutting it down again. Even the people closest to us, with whom we have to work, are changing for the worse too. The older publishers, still not quite extinct, wanted to serve genius and talent; they tried to find for their lists some authors in whom they believed; and sometimes such authors were subsidised for years. But most publishers now think in terms not of authors and their careers but of individual books, not of a list built up for years but of the immediate best-seller. The question is not "Where is the talent that must be carefully nursed?" but "Where is the book, whoever writes it, that might hit the jack-pot?" In America—and what is true of America today will probably be true of England tomorrow—there are publishers who would not know a real book even if they could read one, who are frankly in the mass production business, suppliers of merchandise that happens to have coloured covers instead of sausage skins, and in the sight of such pulp merchants an author hardly exists at all, except as a provider of 'titles'. So the emphasis has passed from the author to individual books, and now from books to 'titles', bought and sold in job lots. Why do we writers receive such disproportionately small royalties on mass-produced paperback books? I think it is because when the publishers are originally budgeting for these things, instead of beginning with the author, the one who created the book, they forget about him until the very end, so that his miserable share is squeezed in at the last moment. And even the old giants of authorship are beginning to have their titles changed and dead naked blondes dumped on their covers, to make them attractive to the mass book trade.

During the last ten years the tide of new books has never ebbed, but where in all this are the names that are house-hold words, the public figures of authorship? Do not tell me there has not been time: ten years are ample. Do not bring in again those giants and dwarfs, for there were apparent giants made out of smaller dwarfs in the past, when the status of authorship was not declining, our pro-fession not shrinking. I will grant an objector only one point, namely that, as a shoddy mass culture increases, some young writers of original talent deliberately widen the gap between themselves and the big public; among so many low of brow, they heighten theirs. This is easily understood, easily forgiven; but it is unwise to erect too many barriers between books and the simpler readers in search of pleasure. Writers who are less anxious to communicate something than they are to keep themselves culturally pure and unspotted are in danger of becoming not only invisible but also inaudible and unintelligible. It is not out of such delicate fabric that recognisable public figures can be cut. Our society, already looking inhuman in some of its aspects, cannot be restored to a full humanity by a small artificial anti-popular culture any more than it can by the mechanical antics of mass amusement. Great art is never vulgar, but, unlike small precious art, it always looks as if it might be, as if a lot of ordinary people had been staring through the doors and windows while it was being created. These people in the street care less than ever about authors and literature; they no longer even remember what a blaze of literary genius this country has known, unlike their grandfathers who may have hardly read a book and yet knew there were great writers in the land. They arrived by excursion to catch a glimpse of Tennyson at Farringford; no motor coaches are seen heading for Chelsea labelled T. S. Eliot. But I think the crowd is neutral rather than hostile. The enemy is to be found among those who control the crowd, who form the power groups, who direct the machinery of mass communication, the hard ambitious types, the smooth official types, the art despisers and life haters. The men of power are cutting us down even when pretending to praise us. Stalin said "Writers are the engineers of the soul," but the emphasis there is on 'engineers'—he believed in engineers. Some of you here—non-members, therefore payers of good money at the door and entitled to one question, may be asking now if we scribblers are not taking ourselves too seriously, over-estimating our importance to the community. To which I would reply at once: Probably, for it is an old bad habit of ours. But then I would add two qualifications. What is struggling to come through our scribble, if we are honest, undefeated, still on fire somewhere, may be of great consequence. And secondly, if this question about importance to the community has any real depth, we too can ask it elsewhere. In the last two weeks I must have seen a hundred pictures, not one of which I wanted to see, showing me two Russian visitors to India, and millions of Hindoos swarming, cheering, throwing flowers, as if Krishna himself had arrived and not two cards that happen to be on top of a rather soiled pack. And if we are putting the brutal question, then—What have these two done for those Hindoos?—or, for that matter, for the rest of us? Yes, we can start asking questions too.

Mark Twain's friend said that everybody complains about the weather but nobody does anything about it. I have tried to show that, for us who write, the whole climate of our time is changing. Does that mean we can do nothing about it? Here I would remind you of what I suggested at the outset, that it is not those of us that acknowledge the unpleasant facts who have lost heart and are in full retreat. Where the line really breaks is where it is supposed to be held, first, by those who smilingly refuse in public to believe that all is not well, but who in fact are secretly afraid of even drawing any conclusion; and secondly, by those who assure us that history always repeats itself (and it doesn't), that everything we say has been said before, that it will all come right because it always has. These are the men who, when their wives announce on the fiftieth occasion that they hear a noise in the dining-room, burrow deeper into the bed-clothes and allow the burglar to pack the silver at his leisure. But what can we writers do, now that our world changes so rapidly, as if moved by vast invisible forces to conform to some new pattern behind the veil? Not much, probably, but nothing at all if we are as much afraid of the immediate situation as all those readers who will no longer welcome a book if it deals with our own time. We can make a start, however, by behaving towards one another—and now I address myself exclusively to fellow writers—*not* as if we all had suites-de-luxe in the *Queen Mary* but as if we had all left the foundering liner in open boats, with no more Cunard Service and Gracious Living but with the North Atlantic darkly heaving and screaming at us. For when nearly everybody else is trying to cut us down, we authors work even harder trying to cut one another down. We may still believe, having a natural inclination that way, that many of our colleagues are impudent charlatans; but we must remember that far more impudent, successful, and dangerous charlatans, who are looking forward to no writing of ours except our final application for a small pension, are enjoying the sight of us carving one another up. Though a fellow writer may have an outlook and vision of things different from our own, if he express them honestly, bravely, and honourably, we should be quick and stout in his defence, thereby upholding our whole profession, and should not help the power-mongers and their hirelings who no longer want any man to do anything honestly, bravely, and honourably.

We must face the sheer economic facts of our situation. The cost of books goes up and up; the number of intelligent book-buyers goes down and down. It is no use our complaining that people seem to think we live on the moon if we behave as if we lived there. The anxiety of those publishers who still want to publish good books, those booksellers who still want to sell good books, is our anxiety. Their final ruin would not leave us very much. The book, even though it should be menaced by policemen muttering about obscenity, is still the citadel of free writing. Now literary publishers and booksellers who still read may not be the most wildly original and creative partners in trading, but if they are considering the widening space between the few who buy books and the many who are limited to libraries, if they should plan to set up a few stalls in that wide space, let us instantly offer our co-operation or even suggest a device or two ourselves, joining forces to meet and master the situation. Because it is easy for us now to feel rather shabby, rather neglected, somewhere in the darker corner of the new picture, it is urgent that we should remember some things. For even if we believe we are merely midgets following giants—and a lurking modesty must not encourage us to be bluffed into cutting ourselves off at the knees—we must not forget we are the successors and colleagues of those giants. The vocation they chose is our chosen vocation too; we know the same compulsions and pains, the same triumphs and joys, of creation. We may not be Shakespeare, but we are a hell of a sight more like him than the zombies and parrots who tell us we're not. It may be a good thing that few of us now attend those banquets at which our Glorious Heritage of English Letters is praised, often by men who would not open a tin of beans for a living author if he were starving. We might lose our temper. But then again, perhaps it is time some temper was lost, some plain words sharply said, some pens given a stabbing point. And here we may have to use, out of sheer self-defence, those very mass communications that are helping to change our society, just because it is impossible now to appeal to a really wide audience in any other way. How much we should use them, how far we can help to civilise them, whether they could ruin us before we improved them— these and similar nice problems I must leave to your individual judgments. But if, as I believe, our world is already dangerously divided between intellect without feeling and feeling without intellect, then it is all the more urgently in need of all that we can give it coming both from the mind and from the heart. We may be required yet, at the eleventh hour, like those psychologists in Los Angeles who keep their illuminated signs flashing all night, ready to cope with a neurosis fresh from a cabaret. However we may regard it, we writers are members of this changing society, and must endure it. That word *endure* reminds me of my favourite quotation, from *King Lear*. We might bear it in mind as we cling to our belief that the art and the craft we practise, the decency and dignity and full humanity of our calling, may yet help the community in its bitterest need, so long as we do not first fail ourselves, so long as we remember to give this speech of Edgar's an even grander meaning than the play intended. So allow me to remind you how, among alarms and retreats, Gloucester enters muttering:

No further, sir; a man may rot even here.

To which his son Edgar cries:

What, in ill thoughts again? Men must endure
Their going hence, even as their coming hither:
Ripeness is all. Come on.